BETWEEN HEAVEN AND EARTH

Recipes for Living and Loving

Other Books by Laura Archera Huxley

You Are Not the Target

This Timeless Moment: A Personal View of Aldous Huxley

Oneadayreason to Be Happy

The Child of Your Dreams
with Dr. Piero Ferrucci

BETWEEN HEAVEN

Recipes for Living and Loving

AND EARTH

Laura Archera Huxley

IN COLLABORATION WITH DR. PIERO FERRUCCI

> The Jade Emperor condescended to take an
> indulgent view. "These creatures in the world
> below," he said, "were compounded of the
> essence of heaven and earth, and nothing that
> goes on there should surprise us."

—Wu Ch'eng-en: *Monkey*
Translated by Arthur Waley

Hay House, Inc.
Santa Monica, CA

BETWEEN HEAVEN AND EARTH
Recipes for Living and Loving
by Laura Archera Huxley

ISBN: 0-937611-87-5
Library of Congress Catalog Card No. 90-80706

91 92 93 94 95 96   10 9 8 7 6 5 4 3 2 1
First Printing, Tradepaper Edition, February 1991

Published and Distributed in the United States by
Hay House, Inc.
501 Santa Monica Boulevard
Post Office Box 2212
Santa Monica, California 90407 USA

Printed in the United States of America
on Recycled Paper

ACKNOWLEDGMENTS

I wrote this book during the most difficult period of my life. Due to a series of irreparable losses, I was struggling between the awareness of life's impersonal, survival-oriented drive and my own personal view that life is not unconditionally desirable, and is worth living only if it has a certain quality. Writing this book would, I felt, restore quality to my life and, I hoped, to the lives of others.

But I would not even have begun this project had I not had, first, the encouragement of my publisher, Roger Straus, and, later, of my collaborator, Dr. Piero Ferrucci. The theoretical and practical knowledge of Piero Ferrucci has been as invaluable as his unfailing good will and brightness, strangely similar to that which so characterized Aldous. I could not have completed this book without the sustaining warmth and skill of several friends who, each in his own unique way, gave of themselves. I would like to acknowledge each one specifically; since it is not possible to do so here, I hope that the reality of my gratitude will carry itself to: Rosabelle Brown, Ram Dass, Kathi de Sainte Colombe, Greta Elgaard, John Ervin, Bernardine Fritz, Ellen Gifford, Dan Hirsh, Sarge Hixcon, Christopher Isherwood, James J. Julian, John and Tony Lilly, Kayla

Mitchell, Roger and Kay Moss, Juan and Kathy (Paula) Pfeiffer, Janice Seaman, Pat Strachan, Betty Wendell— and to little Karen Pfeiffer, for reminding me of the silent, clear space where Buddha smiles. May she never forget it.

An especially loving thought goes to my close associates, Marjorie Hall and Marie Le Put, for their practical and intuitive cooperation.

To Ginny Pfeiffer
in homage to
her exquisitely subtle essence and humor,
her perceptive, imperceptible leadership
and its quickening influence in my life,
her unique way of loving and being compassionate—
practical   undemanding   weightless.
L.A.H.

CONTENTS

FOREWORD *by Ram Dass* · *1*

INTRODUCTION: Our Spiraling Consciousness · 3

PROLOGUE TO THE RECIPES · 11

Part One

WILL, IMAGINATION, BODY · 27

DAYDREAMING · 51

"HAD YOU KNOWN HOW TO SUFFER . . ." · 57

BETWEEN HEAVEN AND EARTH · 67

YOUR SIGNATURE, PLEASE · 75

YES–NO–YES · 79

Part Two

NUTRITION, TRANSFORMER OF CONSCIOUSNESS · 104

Personal Relationship with Food · 111

Buying Food: Quality and Quantity · 113

The Preparation of Food · 117

Vibrations · 118

Diet and Supplements · 121

Fasting · 125

Oxygen · 130

THE COOKING META TOY · 141

Meta Toy One · 145

Meta Toy Two · 151

Meta Toys One and Two · 154

Roulette · 158

Making a Cooking Meta Toy · 160

Part Three

ALL LIVING IS RELATIONSHIP: Invitation · 166

RELATIONSHIP WITH ONESELF · 168

Be Your Own Ideal Parents · 168

Mystery Suspended among Infinities · 174

RELATIONSHIP WITH OTHERS · 185

A Moving Sea · 185

The Cruelty of Unawareness · 188

Our Instant Reactions · 192

Play with Dynamite · 197

Facts and Feelings · 202

Ignoring · 205

Slave and Master: Identity Lost and Repossessed · 207

Vendetta · 212

Possessiveness · 216

Silent One-Candle Dinner · 219

Be a Birth Giver · 222

We Are All Magicians · 227

Conclusion: Pastime Games · 230

Part Four

DEFEATED FROM THE BEGINNING · 238

YOUR EVER-RECEPTIVE CONFIDANT · 241

NOW I WANT TO DO PROPELLERS: Express Series · 245

FROM ANOTHER PLANET · 261

LIKE A TIGER IN THE JUNGLE · 265

SEA-SKY PAINTING · 273

OUR BODY OF LIGHT · 283

BREATHE MORE, EAT LESS, LOVE MORE: An Epicurean
Recipe · 294

Appendix One: PROJECT SANITY · 309

Appendix Two: PROJECT CARESSING · 313

Suggested Reading · 317

FOREWORD

by Ram Dass

In *Between Heaven and Earth*, as in her previous books, Laura Huxley speaks simply at many levels. She touches us aesthetically, intellectually, practically, psychologically and spiritually. Her balancing of these diverse aspects of life is a teaching from which most of us can repeatedly profit.

In the course of our many years of close friendship, Laura, more than any other person, has reminded me of that balance. Whether the reminder comes as a wildflower resting on the front page of the newspaper, a few strawberries set on the desk by my writing material, the "Meta toy" at lunch, the mystic vision discussed at the automobile garage, the jars of vivid "garbage art" over the sink, the emotionally disturbed client on the phone being introduced to mega vitamin therapy while a Corelli concerto fills the house, or an intense discussion of the history of man's spiritual search while walking with the dog in dense underbrush atop a tiny mountain in Hollywood, Laura teaches me again and again that "grace-full" living is keeping it all together, here, there, and beyond.

I have recommended Laura's previous books to thousands of people in recent years and it is with a happy heart that I introduce those of you who have not yet had your life touched by my friend to this superb blend of heart, mind, and soul that is Laura Huxley.

—*Ram Dass*,
New York

Man is as divine as nature,
as infinite as the void.

—Aldous Huxley
  Island

INTRODUCTION
Our Spiraling Consciousness

Inhabitants of that captivating, unpredictable space between heaven and earth, we are not fully earthly like animals—for how soon in life, thanks to our conditioning, we lose our animal grace!—nor are we, as yet, heavenly beings. The simplest proof is that I am writing this and you are reading it. Animals and angels are not, as far as I know, particularly interested in the printed word.

Poised between heaven and earth we still retain precious primal instincts for survival and pleasure; we have not evolved into actualized gods, yet we are endowed with vast knowledge and tremendous powers for good and evil. Due to our nature, both animal and divine, we find ourselves in situations which every day become more complex, more puzzling, at times seeming insoluble. The purpose of these recipes for living and loving is to stimulate in our multiple nature a keener insight and a realization that our conflicting characteristics are desirable advantages rather than burdens. Aldous called us multiple amphibians who, privileged to live in several worlds, all too often get trapped in one of them only, and usually not one of our choice. When do we have the privilege of *conscious* choice? Rarely. We are influenced by a myriad of unconscious needs and desires, by surroundings that bombastically or imperceptibly influence our chemistry, our intellect, our emotions—and therefore our decisions.

Experiencing the recipes for living and loving will increase our capacity to appreciate and cooperate with various energies emanating from heaven and earth. These energies are continually interpenetrating and transforming each other. Physicists and mystics understand this fluidity and agree that there is nothing final about us; we are continuously changing and becoming. How much of the changing process is within our power to influence? I shall not attempt to answer that basic question. All the books in the world would not be as valid and potent as our own decisive answer. It is up to us to decide to what extent we want to influence our process of change. It is our own *deeper self* that has to make that vital decision: when to accept a state of being and when to change it. Who is this *deeper self?* We probably know already, and experiencing the recipes for living and loving will be instrumental in our knowing more deeply.

Many recipes stimulate realization that it is the synchronization of will, imagination and body that gives high quality to our life, harmony to our vibrations. We feel that much confusion is due to the division of these capital elements in our lives: WILL, IMAGINATION, BODY. Their balanced unity forms a triangle of unsuspected power, which gives immediate, tangible rewards. To our knowledge the reality and authority of this triangle has not been sufficiently brought to light.

If we grind our teeth, stop breathing, freeze our muscles in an effort of will, we are not as effective as if we loose our jaws, free our muscles, and breathe harmoniously. The conscious use of these functions in cooperation with, not against, our deep will, sometimes releases the power of revelation. We are then in direct contact with the source of life often obstructed by corrosive influences. Releasing life's flow is the purpose of these recipes.

"All Living Is Relationship" is dedicated to our fundamental issue: relationship with self, with others and with the expanding universe. How do we treat the universe on each side of our skin?

In "Nutrition, Transformer of Consciousness" we direct our attention to the influence that our choice of and relationship with food has on our consciousness and therefore on our life. The "Cooking Meta Toy" takes us into the kitchen, where we feel the earthly energies of food. Such energies are so outreaching and self-evident as to make it obvious that vegetables, grains and fruits have powers and value beyond, as well as within, their chemical analysis. The preparation of food can awaken a deeper reverence for life, a feeling which is in itself very nutritious. The pure pleasure of pure food is a joyful act of sensual awareness.

Other recipes will make us aware that there is much more to ourselves than the body we see. We are also a vibrational body, sometimes called the aura or *Body of Light,* which we can contact, enjoy and expand. Vibrations are the stuff we are made of, and on their quality depends the quality of our lives and relationships.

All the recipes will emphasize the fact that no matter how great our resources and our worldly accomplishments there is no hope for even the slightest progress for us as persons, or as a society, until we stop hurting each other— whether with words, facts or projected thoughts, whether with blind rage or righteous feelings, whether in mass wars or personal relationships. Only a change in our thinking-feeling level can solve our personal problems and, consequently, the problems of relationship whose magnitude increases in proportion to the very means (technology and wealth) we anticipated to be their solution.

We are responsible not only for our actions, but also for our innermost feelings, thoughts and desires; their influence is more far-reaching than we ever realized. For example:

> With the power of our will we can produce physical action. The eminent British neurophysiologist Dr. Grey Walter reported in his 1969 Eddington Memorial Lecture: "Harnessed to an electric machine, by an effort of will, one can influence external events without movement or overt action through the *impalpable* electric surges of one's own brain." In this experiment the subject is viewing TV. Electrodes attached to his scalp transmit his electrical brain activity through an amplifier to the TV. If the subject presses a button, a scene will appear on the screen. But after a while it is sufficient for the subject *to will* to see the scene: the scene appears without his pressing the button. The electrical surge in his brain is sufficient to trigger a switch and make the scene appear. This is called auto-start. "Auto-start can be combined with auto-stop so that the subject can acquire a picture by willing its appearance on the TV screen, and then erase it as soon as he has completed his inspection of it."*

> Plants flourish or wither as reaction to thoughts, feelings and desires directed at them—even at a distance. They thrive when music by Bach or Indian Ragas performed by Ravi Shankar are played for them. They languish and degenerate if bombarded by acid rock.**

* *The Roots of Coincidence*, Arthur Koestler. Random House, 1972.
** *The Secret Life of Plants*, Peter Tompkins and Christopher Bird. Harper & Row, 1973.

A mother rabbit, ashore, reacts at the exact moment that her baby rabbits are killed, despite their being housed on a submarine and separated from her by tons of water.*

These and scores of similar experiments exemplify the interdependence of life. More and more the observations of physicists and mystics are in agreement: we are all living in "the great sea of being" through which we continuously communicate and influence each other and our environment. Any injurious thought, feeling, action tarnishes that sea of being in which and from which we all live. Christ said, "What you do to the least of them, you do to me." The pollution of water, food and air comprises only the visible portion of a threatening iceberg. Its hidden foundation is the deeper and graver pollution of our consciousness on which *everything* else depends.

Experts tell us that the human race is on the brink of disaster: is it possible that only such an emergency can awaken the vast resources lying dormant in our being? It is generally agreed that we use less than a tenth of our intellectual endowment. What about our spiritual endowment? How much of it do we use? Are we aware of its magnetic energy? Does our education enliven our capacities for compassion, love, joy and their pervading power? The recipes designed as a form of self-education focus on that power and on its all-embracing reach.

Many of us feel that an evolutionary quickening, an ongoing transmutation into another level of consciousness is taking place. This, it is thought, will solve problems that could not be solved on the same level at which they were produced.

* *Psychic Discoveries Behind the Iron Curtain,* Sheila Ostrander and Lynn Schroeder. Prentice-Hall, Inc., 1970.

"There is not a single problem in the world today," says Ram Dass (Dr. Richard Alpert), ". . . starvation, overpopulation, integration, ecological pollution . . . that would not change were the consciousness of mankind to change."

We trust the recipes for living and loving will nourish the flow of our spiraling consciousness.

Aldous often warned us of the intellectual sin of generalization; but I caught him committing that sin! He would say:

> *"One never loves enough."*

PROLOGUE TO THE RECIPES

As you begin these recipes for living and loving, imagine that you are a being from another galaxy. You have just landed on Earth and this book falls into your hands. To you all is fresh and possible.

Where is our spiraling consciousness taking us? Who knows? Let the recipes for living and loving be a free ticket for cosmic traveling—you may find yourself in known lands or in unexplored places; you may find the center of the cosmos on the palm of your hand or in an unimagined space; you may visit enchanted shores and discover that they are part of your everyday walk.

Einstein is considered one of the world's greatest abstract thinkers—yet he pointed out that only experience can give us knowledge of reality. He couldn't have expressed it more forcibly than when he said,

"PURE LOGICAL THINKING CANNOT YIELD US A KNOWLEDGE OF THE EMPIRICAL WORLD: ALL KNOWLEDGE OF REALITY STARTS FROM EXPERIENCE AND ENDS WITH IT. PROPOSITIONS ARRIVED AT BY PURELY LOGICAL MEANS ARE COMPLETELY EMPTY OF REALITY."

Not by just reading the recipes but by carrying them out and experiencing them, you discover their reality in relationship to yours.

I have made a recording of a few recipes.* I suggest you do the same: it is an effective way to experience those recipes which are difficult to memorize. You will find it easier to do some of the recipes by following the recording made for you, by you, at your own tempo.

* "Recipes for Living & Loving," by Laura Huxley, 1540 Washburn Road, Pasadena, Calif. 91105.

Frequently there is more than one type of direction in a recipe, the reason being that different levels of consciousness are reached by different types of direction.

Throughout this book we use the expressions "he," "him," "his" instead of "he/she," "him/her," "his/hers." We do this to avoid burdening the reader and offending her/him with obvious explanations.

In the following recipes we will use the words "toxic feeling" or "toxicity," meaning poison, as generalizations to simplify communication. It is difficult to know exactly the way in which each of us experiences a "bad" feeling. Some of us feel it mainly emotionally, some almost exclusively on the physical level. On either level these feelings are variously called: rage, resentment, frustration, tension, sadness, despair, sense of justice, hatred, unrequited love, pain, etc. Or they may be felt as indigestion, stiff joints, heart trouble, liver upset, cancer, diabetes, cold, schizophrenia, etc. It would be presumptuous for us to give a name to your feeling, so let us agree that, when we speak about toxicity or toxic feelings or sensations, we mean those feelings from which you choose to set yourself free.

It is impossible for a human being to be totally free of programming. Nature, our genetic heritage, and nurture—air, food, water, people and culture—dovetail into each other. To avoid being programmed, a child would have to be kept in solitary confinement—and this would kill him. Seven hundred years ago Frederick II, Holy Roman Emperor, conducted an experiment to determine what language children would grow up to speak if they had never heard a single word spoken. Would they speak Hebrew (then thought to be the oldest tongue), Greek, Latin or the language of their parents? He instructed foster mothers and nurses to feed and bathe the children but under no circumstances to speak or prattle to them. The experiment failed, for every one of the children died. So let us abandon the idea of living without programming of any sort. The programming of which we want to be freed is that which prevents the development of our desirable characteristics and talents.

The recipes for living and loving are designed to stimulate an awareness of that part of our programming which was and is imposed upon us without our conscious acceptance and knowledge. They are tools to help us put a space between the programming and our uncontaminated Self. As this space becomes more real we can observe our programming dispassionately and objectively. We will *know when we have become an objective observer of our programming, for then there will no longer be inner dialogue such as: "There, you did it again! . . . You should not, you should not. . . . Don't be stupid. . . . I told you so. . . ." As this inner dialogue becomes fainter we will be able to choose for ourselves a conscious programming harmonious with our being and our view of life. Conscious self-programming generally obliterates destructive and unconscious programming. The important point is that self-programming is our own decision.*

*There was the Age of Reason and the Age of Enlighten-
ment, the Age of Faith, of Reformation, of Progress. What
will historians call the second part of the twentieth century? A fitting name would be the "Age of Audacity."*

*Ours is a time of selfless daring, as well as shameless
bumptiousness. The dictionary gives two meanings to
"audacity": (1) Boldness, daring, and (2) Impudence,
shamelessness, disregard of law and decency. The syno-
nyms for "audacity" are just as contradictory: spirit,
bravery, valor, bold originality—or insolence, indiscretion, effrontery.*

*We all know of acts and persons of high daring and
valor. We also know of action and persons of insolent
indiscretion, spurred by cowardice rather than daring.
There are many ways to be audacious in the noble sense:*

Say something about which you are embarrassed or
ashamed.

Speak to someone of whom you are afraid.

(Record your own noble example.)

And there are also many ways to fulfill the derogatory meaning of "audacity":

Talk aloud in a quiet place.

Interrupt a serious talker with an unnecessary or insignificant remark.

Perform some indiscreet action just to attract attention.

(Record your own derogatory example.)

With the retrospect of passing time or, better still, right now, let us glimpse the role we played in the Age of Audacity. Which meaning of the word "audacity" do you choose for your life in this age? As you experience the recipes for living and loving, your choice will clearly emerge.

Part One

WILL, IMAGINATION, BODY

I.

Please read this recipe sitting in a chair with your legs crossed so that one leg is dangling freely over the other at the knee joint.

> *Let your leg swing: we often do this without even realizing it.*
>
> *Now, will your foot to kick. Notice how the quality of the movement changes into a neutral, will-directed action.*
>
> *Now, without changing position, continue the same movement, but imagine that you are kicking a ball. See how different the movement is, now that your will-directed imagination has taken charge of your leg muscles.*
>
> *Now the leg is no longer kicking the ball—it is kicking the most obnoxious person or situation or feeling. It is kicking the very thing you do not want in your inner or outer world. It may be some unimportant, boring little thing, or it may be the very impediment that blocks your life.*
>
> Give direction to your imagination with great power and decisiveness. Imagine that what you are kicking is right there at the point of your foot, and hit it squarely in the middle. If you cannot visualize it, just feel it in your foot, in your leg, in your whole body. And now kick it far away again and again—get rid of it. Realize: your life will

*change if you can kick that impediment away—kick until
you are exhausted and free.*

What happened in these four seemingly similar but
actually different movements? The first one was done by
your body automatically. The second was consciously directed by your will. In the third and fourth movements
we used the will and imagination to direct the body. In
the fourth movement the imagination awoke deep, powerful feelings which involved the reaction of the sympathetic
nervous system. This ancient instinctual mechanism,
thanks to which we survive, mobilized our reserve of
adrenalin, increased the rate of breathing and rushed the
blood to the muscles. Our kicking became much more significant and strong. Compare it to the first kicking which
is only muscular and does not involve conscious will or
imagination.

*Now stand up. Raise your arm, and reach with your hand
to as high a point as possible. With the fingertip of the
middle finger, you are reaching higher and higher. This
is a muscular, neutral action, directed by the will. You
stretch as much as you can.*

*Now, imagine that there are some grapes, high up there.
You stretch but you cannot reach them. Those grapes are
beautiful, very tasty. Try to reach them, first on tiptoe;
then you might even want to make a little jump. It would
be a waste to leave those grapes up there, and it is so hot.
Try, try again—another jump and the grapes are in your
hand. Feel the roundness, that gentle weight—you are
anticipating that fresh pleasure. Then you feel the contact first with your lips, then with your tongue. Roll one
grape in your mouth; enjoy its roundness with your whole
mouth for a while. Then press it on your palate and feel
the sweet explosion when the peel breaks and the very*

essence is released. Your tongue is exploring texture and taste.

Did you notice in the first part of this stretching exercise, when you just moved your body, how different the feeling was from the second part, when you moved your body while imagining the grapes?

Now: Wait! Don't sit down again! Before reading further than page 30, go out and run. Is it too cold? Too hot? You don't feel like running? You might do it some other time, but first you want to read past this to see what it is all about? Don't! This is not a book to be merely read: it is a collection of recipes to be experienced.

Now, you are going to mobilize a little more of your will. You are doing something that requires a little bit of effort. It is beautiful to be able to mobilize energy, which will then be at your disposal.

Go out of your house now, and start running, or at least walking very fast. Once again, it is the will that directs your physical acts. Now you rest a moment, and then start running again. But this time you are running away from something. A giant ten feet tall, with a big stick in his hands, is running after you, and you run for your life. Stop again, look backwards: the giant is not there. It was all your imagination, of course, but how did that change the way you ran: not only the speed, but the quality, the flavor, so to speak, of your running?

Now you are going to run again; actually you would like to stop because you are tired, and this is really too much, and so on. You hear a choir of protests from different parts of your body and also from your commonsense mind. Sometimes it is very important to listen to this choir, and get to know each one of the singers. This time, you decide to ignore it. Stop a moment, and let go of all habits, thoughts, of all physical discomforts, aches and pains, shortcomings, chronological age, etc., with which you have identified yourself every day—alas—every hour of your life. Stop and drop all of that burden for just a few moments. Now you are going to walk or run as a pure spirit—don't ask how, but something is going to run you —and you are moving effortlessly and lightly toward a chosen ideal. At that turn of the road or at that tree one of these ideals will be explicably, intensely and fully present.

Choose one:
> serenity
> lightness
> tenderness
> gratefulness
> beauty
> understanding
> love

Run to it!

The quality of your running will change, even though the muscular action may remain the same. And your total attitude will probably change too.

Go out now and do these different kinds of running, and when you come back we will discuss it together.

For those of you who are *really* in a situation where running is *impossible* (health, location, people), do the following recipe:

> Lie down on the floor, or on a large bed. You will need a wide space.

> Curl up so as to take as little space as possible—knees touching your face, arms around your knees. This is generally called the fetal position. Imagine that you are so small you could easily be in your mother's womb—and then become even smaller. You are getting to be the smallest thing you can imagine. You become so tiny that

you almost disappear. You are so extraordinarily tiny that naturally you, as well as everyone else, are duly impressed by it. In fact, you think of yourself and are addressed as "Your Royal Tininess."

Your Royal Tininess now enjoys and basks in your royal tininess for as long as it pleases Your Royal Tininess. Then Your Royal Tininess begins to count aloud. At the count of ONE, Your Royal Tininess starts to move and grow; at TWO, your body unfolds and opens; at THREE there is no trace of tininess left. You are wide open, already larger than your everyday self. At FOUR, your arms and legs are pushing through the walls. At FIVE, you are so unbelievably vast that your toes and fingertips tickle anything you choose in the universe. You naturally think of yourself and are addressed as "Your Royal Vastness."

Your Royal Vastness enjoys and basks in its royal vastness. It is comfortable and real to be Your Royal Vastness. The part that is the most enjoyable is being comfortable in both of those extreme kingdoms of yours. "The Kingdom of Tininess" and "The Kingdom of Vastness."

Now you are going to count down five to one, and become again Your Royal Tininess. At FIVE, Your Royal Vastness feels a pull at the center of itself, and your arms and legs become short enough to be contained in the room. At FOUR, your body is its everyday size, but at THREE, it is already gently folding as do some flowers at dusk. At TWO, it is very small, the arms embracing the knees, which are pulled up to the face. And at ONE, you reach the delightful Kingdom of Your Royal Tininess. You deserve your royal title, for you are the Tiniest Thing that ever lived. It is hard to believe that you were at one time (but when was that?) Your Royal Vastness! Your Royal Tininess enjoys and basks in your royal tininess for as long as Your Royal Tininess wishes.

Go from one kingdom to the other several times, enjoying them both and the fabulous trips from one to the other. This trip usually takes five minutes of our clock time, but you do it on your own inner rhythm. The trip between your two kingdoms may be the most valuable part of the recipe because you can, if you wish, be aware of each part of yourself changing in this extreme way. You can make this one your daily recipe and become more and more aware of the tremendous capacities of your WILL, IMAGINATION and BODY.

End as Your Royal Vastness. I suggest this because it is better to conclude the recipe with your lungs wide open. When you get up from the floor you may perceive the furniture and objects of your room to be small and distant as though seen through the wrong end of binoculars.

Variation One:

This is a variation only in rhythm, in which you change from Your Royal Tininess to Your Royal Vastness in a matter of seconds. Before starting this variation, review in your mind all the movements that you did previously when you were going from one kingdom to the other at a slow pace. Now you are going to do the same thing as if it were a movie sequence accelerated to the extreme.

Lie down and as fast as you can, and as many times as you can, BE:

> Your Royal Tininess
> Vastness
> Tininess
> Vastness
> Tininess
> Vastness
> Tininess
> Vastness
> Tininess
> Vastness

Stop when an exhilarating sensation comes over you.

The fast rhythm changes the character of the recipe; it is as if you explode into Your Royal Vastness and implode into Your Royal Tininess. When you explode into Royal Vastness, and implode into Royal Tininess, and explode into Royal Vastness, keep in touch with the details of the movements and sensations as when you were doing this slowly. End with the explosion. It is good to do this in bed when you are ready for sleep. Let the explosion take you directly into dream country.

Variation Two:

Now surprise yourself—do this recipe alternating the fastest and slowest rhythms you can master, but don't let yourself know when you are going to change. You are stretching your muscles into vastness or retracting them into tininess with the slow, round, rubbery motion of an astronaut in outer space . . . and suddenly you shift into a lightning speed while doing the same motions—*what a surprise!*

Variation Three:

This is basically the same as the main recipe except that you add the magic of your voice to the transformation.

Choose the rhythm you prefer for traveling from one kingdom to the other; as you do so, harmonize your trip with your voice. Your voice may be high and tiny when in the kingdom of tininess, and deep and loud in your kingdom of vastness—but who knows? It may be just the opposite, or something totally unpredictable.

Find your real voice for each kingdom and carry the

sound from one to the other, adapting the pitch and the volume to each. By using synchronously your will, imagination and body to their fullest extent, you can make this your master recipe.

Now that you have experienced these recipes, let's discuss what happened. First of all, you used your will, increasing it with each of the three experiments. The will started each single thing that you did. This made you feel like the conscious director of your actions and energies. You used your imagination, and this gave a new significance to each of the experiments performed. You used your body, and this made the "juices flow." Your blood reached more cells in your body than it was reaching before, your glands became more activated, some dormant energy was discharged and, most important, your whole system was oxygenated. You were more alive and felt more real because you used consciously and synchronously Will, Imagination, Body. You experienced the surprising power of integration. We symbolize this integrated functioning with an equilateral triangle:

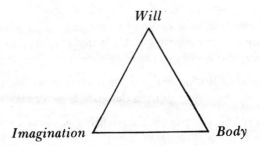

In the first part of the three experiments—when we just kicked, just stretched, just ran—we used only body and will. In the second part of the three experiments—when we kicked a projection of our feelings; stretched to get grapes and ate them; ran away from and toward something or traveled from the Kingdom of Tininess to the Kingdom of Vastness—we also used our imagination. The triangle of full power and total functioning was formed.

At this point you may ask: What are the practical advantages of being aware of this $\underset{I \quad B}{\triangle}^{W}$?

The answer is that we can use everyday actions, often
tiring or unsettling, to align our scattered energies. By
consciously using the power of the will, imagination and
body, we transform necessary, but at times seemingly
futile, actions in a creative and often amusing way.

In each person's life there are chores which must be
done; being habitual, these chores tend to lower our
awareness.

The use of $\underset{I \quad B}{\triangle}^{W}$ wakes us up.

For instance, when you shower:

> *Those thousands of droplets not only clean your skin,
> they also give a lively sprinkle to that cherished project of
> yours that is still in its budding state.*

> *Think of that project as newly planted grass: through the
> brown earth you can see the grass beginning to sprout.*

> *As you shower you see the tenderly green blades enjoying
> the droplets as your skin does.*

> *Your body is refreshed and strengthened after your
> shower, and your budding project has more vitality, more
> direction.*

When you clean your house:

> *Sweep and clean not only the visible dust, but use your
> imagination to sweep away those particles of psycho-emo-
> tional dust that obscure the sparkling quality of life—dust
> in the house, dust in the mind, dust in the heart. Directed*

by an act of will, your body and imagination sweep and dust with free, aware movement—gradually, as your cleaning job progresses, so does the clarity of your bodymind.

As you are doing this inner and outer cleaning it almost becomes a dance. "A dance every time I do house cleaning?" Yes, a new dance every day. A dance during which your bodymind regenerates because, like your house, it is freeing itself from graying dust.

When you have finished cleaning make an empty space on a table or another surface. Feel a correspondingly empty space within yourself. Put a flower, leaf, vegetable, fruit or any other beautiful object on that empty space— inside? outside? Who knows? Beauty in Empty Space: you have created it by sweeping and dusting—inside? outside? Who knows . . .?

After you have repeatedly experienced a number of these recipes you may want to read the following pages in which we discuss the basic elements of the triangle: Will, Imagination, Body. Each of these is an immense subject that cannot be covered in this *book of doing*. However, after we do the recipes it is sometimes useful to look into the principles underlying them. We hope the following inquiry will inspire your individual recipe for the integration of Will, Imagination, Body.

II.

The will is a continuum. In the vegetable and animal realm the will is *instinct* whose command is survival, both for the individuals and for the species. Therefore, nutrition and reproduction are the main necessities. In humans the instinctual will is present (or we would not be alive), but its demands have evolved. Inventiveness in art, music and technology; egotism and philanthropy; greed and compassion; love of many types and levels—these and other human traits are inspired and supported by the will to survive. For us survival is not simply physical: even when our physical needs are fulfilled, *we* are not—for we need love, self-expression, understanding and communication. Our will is to survive, not only physically, but emotionally, intellectually and psychologically as well.

Moreover, even when those needs are satisfied, there is often an urge in human beings for something greater than what has been achieved by our personal will. At a certain point of a person's evolution, will power seems to want to give itself up for something greater than itself—for a glimpse of the divine. "Thy will, not mine, be done." Sometimes this cry is uttered in desperation, when we no longer have faith in our earthly capacity and long for something heavenly. Other times, it is the last step to liberation, the final flight from the golden yet limiting palace of personal will.

The will can be imagined as a continuously evolving spectrum of sounds and colors—slower and deeper vibration beginning in past eternity and ascending in ever finer vibration into future eternity.

In this immense journey of the will where do we find ourselves? Each of us must give his answer to this all-embracing question.

The nature of the will has always been the subject of much controversy. The social situation and cultural climate of the first part of this century conferred the highest position upon the unyielding, intransigent will. It has been called the Victorian Will—a willing in which the wholeness of the individual is neglected, his many facets disregarded. The aims are chosen from the outside, without taking into consideration a person's inner needs and powers of imagination and body. Having given up years of energy—often health and freedom—to the willful, dogged pursuit of a goal, the individual often feels empty-handed and alone when he achieves it. Victorian Will enables us to control our actions—but who controls our imagination, thoughts and feelings? Like wild and restless creatures they are left to exist and fight on the only possible battlefield: our body.

It is not the Victorian Will that governs those bodily functions that keep us alive: heartbeat, food absorption and assimilation, the miraculous balancing of hormones, on which our life and its quality depend. These and other functions are greatly influenced by our imagination, mostly without our conscious will.

The gap between generations has been due in great

measure to a different view of the will. Having seen their parents become slaves of their Victorian Will and of their determination to acquire material success and status, young people have rebelled against will and determination. For many of the older generation who worked their way "up," lack of status and money had been painful; they are determined to spare their children the same deprivation. No wonder so many persons in the middle years are frustrated and bitter to find that hard work and self-control have brought them ulcers, arthritis, heart conditions and a general malaise. As though this were not enough, the children look down on their parents' efforts and grow more distant, sometimes hostile and rebellious.

Mere rebellion against other people's will does not automatically confer will power on the rebel—but unfortunately it gives him that illusion. A clarifying question for a rebel is: are my actions dictated by a genuine deep will—or are they a desperate *reaction* against the blind willing of others? In many instances rebellion against inflexible willing induces a letting go of purpose, determination and finally even the sense of direction. To avoid the Scylla of blind self-pushing and self-punishing, the rebel falls prey to the Charybdis of boredom, uncertainty and "existential vacuum": he has abdicated his will. Abdicated in favor of what? Often it is in favor of the forces of commercial, political or religious propaganda. Sometimes he abdicates his will to disturbed and corrupted individuals by whom he is dominated and taken advantage of. Obviously one of the most important aspects of having an alive and well-functioning will is preventing other people or "impersonal forces" (advertising, subliminal propaganda, etc.) from directing and commanding us. Even more damaging, our own inner destructive forces may take over and paralyze us with depression, apathy, feelings of inadequacy—in short, with deadly toxicity.

But there is another type of willing which is neither the iron will of the Victorian nor the rebellious or apathetic reaction to it. I call this the Attentive Will, and it is described in the following Chinese parable. The knife, representing the wise cook's will, glides through the fluctuation of living, symbolized by the cutting of the ox. The will is not isolated from the rest of the individual's characteristics. As the wise cook says: "My whole being apprehends."

Cutting Up an Ox

Prince Wen Hui's cook
Was cutting up an ox.
Out went a hand,
Down went a shoulder,
He planted a foot,
He pressed with a knee,
The ox fell apart
With a whisper,
The bright cleaver murmured
Like a gentle wind.
Rhythm! Timing!
Like a sacred dance,
Like "The Mulberry Grove,"
Like ancient harmonies!

"Good work!" the Prince exclaimed,
"Your method is faultless!"
"Method?" said the cook,
Laying aside his cleaver.
"What I follow is Tao
Beyond all methods!

"When I first began
To cut up oxen

I would see before me
The whole ox
All in one mass.

"After three years
I no longer saw this mass,
I saw the distinctions.

"But now, I see nothing
With the eye. My whole being
Apprehends.
My senses are idle. The spirit
Free to work without plan
Follow its own instinct
Guided by natural line,
By the secret opening, the hidden space,
My cleaver finds its own way.
I cut through no joint, chop no bone.

"A good cook needs a new chopper
Once a year—he cuts.
A poor cook needs a new one
Every month—he hacks!

"I have used this same cleaver
Nineteen years.
It has cut up
A thousand oxen.
Its edge is as keen
As if newly sharpened.

"There are spaces in the joints;
The blade is thin and keen:
When this thinness
Finds that space
There is all the room you need!
It goes like a breeze!
Hence I have this cleaver nineteen years
As if newly sharpened!

"True, there are sometimes
Tough joints, I feel them coming,

I slow down, I watch closely,
Hold back, barely move the blade,
And whump! the part falls away
Landing like a clod of earth.

"Then I withdraw the blade,
I stand still
And let the joy of the work
Sink in.
I clean the blade
And put it away."

Prince Wen Hui said,
"This is it! My cook has shown me
How I ought to live
My own life!"

This type of Attentive Will, represented by the cook's words and action, is as distant from the Victorian Will as it is from the rebellious or apathetic will which it often triggers.

The will has been compared to a charioteer, a conductor, a choreographer. But the will has not only horses, musicians and dancers to coordinate and inspire. It has a much vaster and subtler kingdom to cultivate, enrich and harmonize: the kingdom of the body and the imagination. The will cannot rule this awesome domain as a despot, but only as a beneficent and attentive leader, inspired and inspiring.

Imagination is not the *talent* of *some* men," said Emerson, who lived to be eighty-three years old, "but the health of every man."

Marcel Proust, who had a melancholic and comparatively short life (forty-five years), had a very different opinion of the imagination: "Often it is the lack of imagination that keeps man from suffering very much."

It is interesting to see how imagination can touch every facet of a human being, and how, when a man talks about it, he gives his beliefs and his biography.

Indeed, one can get a fairly good look inside a person by just asking, "What do you feel about imagination?" Take, for instance, the great Zen Master Ten Shan, who said to a disciple: "Allow one flash of imagination to cross your mind, and lo, you are lost!" Let us take another leap, and see what Oscar Wilde has to say about imagination:

"And there was silence in the House of Judgment. And the Man came naked before God. And God opened the Book of Life of the Man." God goes on to recount all the sins of the Man written therein. The Man had been guilty of practically all sin, including cruelty, lack of charity, thievery, ingratitude, disloyalty, lust and lack of love. To all these charges, the Man answered, "Even so did I." Thereupon God closed the Book of the Life of the Man and said, "Surely I will send you to hell." The Man said he could not do so, because hell was where he had always lived. So then God said He would send him to heaven, and the Man cried out, "Thou canst not!" And God said, "Wherefore can I not send thee to heaven?" And the Man answered, "Because never, and in no place, have I been able to imagine it." And there was silence in the House of Judgment.*

We are not disembodied beings, nor are we shapeless energy, nor unsubstantial images. We have a body, and

---

* *The Poems and Fairy Tales of Oscar Wilde.* Modern Library, Random House.

we live in and through it. And how complex and still un-explained our body is! Even the simple movement of closing and opening a hand involves a complicated series of chemical and electrical events. "To effect a harmonious muscular movement, a thousand minute chemical compounds have to be made *simultaneously* in every *one* of the cells."* Moreover, even a very simple act of imagination will cause complicated bodily processes to occur.

> Sit comfortably and close your eyes. Imagine that you are on the highest skyscraper in the world. You are on its very top, on a terrace. This terrace has no railings. You move toward the edge of the terrace; you look down at the street, and there you see very, very small cars and people. The least movement, and you may fall on that distant, hard cement.

What was the physical effect of this image? Probably, even if you are quite comfortably sitting in the armchair, a wave of vertigo ran through your body; the skyscraper was imaginary, but the vertigo was real.

What are the mysterious processes that connect our extraordinary bodily organism with those intangible, fleeting images, which we can produce for a moment in our mind? We do not know. We would like to know but we do not *need* to know. For the purpose of our recipes it is enough to remember that most of our bodily reactions are directed by our glandular system, and that our glandular system responds to emotion, whether the emotion is induced by actual facts or by imagination.

In the first recipe when we were kicking, we were kick-

---

* *Exhaustion: Causes and Treatment*, Sam E. Roberts, M.D. Rodale Books, 1967.

ing only air, and not the event or person we disliked, but our psychophysical organism reacted in various ways (increased heartbeat, adrenalin release, etc.), *as if* the real person or event were there. When we were actually sitting in our armchair, the imagined fact of being atop a skyscraper gave us vertigo and fear. Likewise, the imaginary grapes made our mouths water, as if they were real. So it is of the utmost importance to remember this chain of events: our glandular system is stimulated by emotions which may be elicited by imagination, by facts or by chemicals. The glandular system so stimulated pours into our bloodstream some of the most powerful substances known: hormones. Regardless of whether the hormones are triggered by imagination or facts or fed by injection, they induce tremendous physical and emotional reactions.*

We can see, then, how powerfully imagination directs our life on all levels. At this time, more than ever in the history of mankind, we must keep in mind the tremendous power of the imagination. Human beings always influenced each other's imagination, but *never has the imagination of so many been at the mercy of so few.* These few are mostly political or industrial leaders, not artists or humanitarians. Never before could one person be seen and heard at the same moment by unimaginable numbers of other human beings. The forces that affect our *imagination*—and therefore our feelings and our lives—are subtle, quick and penetrating. The impact of the media, with its abundance of stimuli intense enough to physio-

* According to Roger Williams's *Free and Unequal* (University of Texas Press, 1953), if a virgin female rat is given the hormone prolactin, she not only will produce milk, but will become very loving and caring for the young, which she usually ignores. She will prepare a nest for them, carry them to it and suckle them.

logically lower our alertness, boggles the imagination. We take out insurance to protect our cars, our homes, our many gadgets, but how many of us take steps to protect our and our children's imagination? Too often children and even infants are fed television—even if it is regurgitating brutality, vulgarity and lies about empty foods and drinks. At such a young age, children are open and have no defense from the all-pervading stimuli of the "boob-tube." Why then are we surprised if they grow up unmanageable and neurotic? It is not difficult to predict that children who absorb murder and vulgarity with their milk will be different from those who are fed beauty and love. It is up to responsible parents and educators to make a conscious choice of imagination-directors and to prevent leaders from fostering destructive programming.

The unification of will, imagination and body has not been given due attention, either in education or in medicine, yet in our age this unification is not just a question of molding a good life, it is a question of survival.

As in any formula, the ingredients of the WIB formula must be in the right proportion and of the highest quality if we want the resulting combination to be palatable. This perfection is not always achieved, and we might want to make some corrections in our psychophysical gastronomy. The will might be automatic and unclear to the consciousness of its owner; it might be blind, badly focused, weak. On the other hand, it might be overriding. Imagination might be impeded and limited: conversely, it might have an overwhelming life of its own and turn to uncontrolled daydreaming. (See recipe entitled "Daydreaming.") The body may have lost that ideal balance between tension and relaxation and be either too explosive or too lethargic.

How do we make an equilateral triangle of WIB? How do we succeed in attaining unbroken, open lines of communication in this triangle? Most of the recipes in this book are designed to actualize these aims.

Realize! The dance of WILL IMAGINATION BODY is not only the dance of harmonious personal life, it is the cosmic dance. . . .

Some of the recipes are carried out better with a supporting partner, others are actually conceived for two persons.
The attitude of the supporting partner is decisive to the
outcome of the recipe. He should not:

> *judge*
> *criticize*
> *interrupt*
> *give opinions*

The two partners must give each other (unless otherwise
agreed before starting) :

> *equal amounts of time*
> *complete freedom of movement*
> *support and empathy rather than sympathy*

When you empathize you understand and feel for the
other person but are not overwhelmed by his emotion and
are able to give support. Sympathy may cause you to feel
so deeply the emotion of the other that you lose your center.

Similarly, when you save someone who is drowning you
feel enough empathy to risk your life for him—yet you
don't let him grab and take you down with him. As sup-

porting partner, let your attitude and action be that of a good swimmer assisting an untrained one: let him swim without help so that he becomes self-reliant; swim nearby so that he knows he will not drown; let him lean on you for a moment to rest—but let him swim on his own most of the time. As the supporting partner, simply be there, fully present. It is your attentive, non-judging presence that gives the other the liberty to rid himself of emotions and fears which may be too anguishing and violent to face alone. This uncritical attitude is necessary to the specific activity of the sustaining partner. In everyday life creative criticism is a necessity for progress.

DAYDREAMING

Daydreaming is frequently mistaken for creative imagination. This recipe focuses on their basic differences. Whereas creative imagination is one of the highest faculties of the human mind, overindulgent daydreaming can drain the human mind. When we direct our imagination we are charioteers leading our horses. When we daydream, we are led by a quarrelsome team of wild horses. By directing our imagination we mold our lives. By daydreaming we feed our fears, our anger, our illusions.

Rarely is daydreaming anything but a dreary reminiscence of bits of past conversation, of unrealistic situations, of unacted desires—a consolation prize for past failures. But the cost of this consolation prize is high, for it steals the energy we need to actualize projects and to solve problems. Daydreaming usurps our ONE AND ONLY NOW.

In the enlightened society of *Island,* Aldous gives paramount importance to training children to direct their imagination, but warns us about daydreaming: "And while you were paying attention . . . you were momentarily delivered from daydreams, from memories, from anticipation, from silly notions."*

* *Island,* Aldous Huxley. Harper & Row, 1962.

Creative imagination combines apparently unrelated elements into new thoughts and actions. It is like the skillful pharmacologist who, by the ingenious combination of chemical compounds, creates a new, perhaps lifesaving, drug. Conversely, daydreaming is a mindless mixing of all kinds of chemicals. Such a careless mixture is dangerous, to say the least.

William Blake expresses the dangers of daydreaming with a power that gives us goose pimples: "Sooner murder an infant in its cradle than nurse unacted desires."

A modern version of daydreaming is watching TV for hours without choosing programs—letting others take over your mind-time-life.

Let's see how planning a dinner party unfolds for the person who uses:

Directed Imagination	Daydreams
Choose the guests.	Choose guests whom one does not have the possibility of inviting.
Invite them.	
Imagine how the guests would best communicate with each other; decide about table seating.	Daydream conversation and behavior of uninvited guests.
Imagine food for the occasion.	Daydream the most delicious *unavailable* food.
Write a list and buy what is needed, etc.	Plan how to cook it in unavailable containers.

The difference between the imaginative doer and the daydreamer is obvious: one fulfills his plans and desires, the other does not. This may not be so important when only a dinner party is involved, but it is extremely important when daydreaming is a way of life, for the day-dreamer is destined to experience failure, frustration and physical exhaustion.

Here is a recipe to stop daydreaming and start creative imagination.

Clarify in your mind the difference between creative imagination and daydreaming.

Experience both. For example: If you experience creative imagination on the subject of "pencil," you might think of a forest from which the wood came, of literature, of drawings. You may have new ideas about writing or drawing.

If you daydream with the subject "pencil," you may immediately think of that note which you would like to have written yesterday to that man or woman who should have written to you before now, and how irritating his behavior is, and what you will write one of these days, and how your point of view will win, and how this note that you will write will be a triumph for you, etc., etc. A great deal of emotion is poured into such daydreaming, and you may be left exhausted by the drained-off energy of your "unacted desire."

Consider many subjects other than the pencil. Experience the different actions and reactions of your bodymind to creative imagination and to daydreaming.

TO CATCH YOURSELF in the ACT of sliding from imagination into daydreaming is the essence of this recipe.

At that moment exhale completely, stay empty and make your entire body very rigid for as long as you can.

Let air in and relax.

Do this three times.

Now direct your attention to the point where you slid into daydreaming. This recipe requires intense energy and concentration. Don't do it for long stretches of time. A few minutes, taken as often as you can, will reveal how your mind works and who is its master.

The following recipe is to be done with a sustaining partner:

Go fully into an orgy of daydreaming.

At the snap of your sustaining partner's fingers, change the subject of your daydreaming. Stop the ongoing daydream and start a new one.

The sustaining partner must snap his fingers at different intervals of time—one minute, forty seconds, seventy seconds—at random. After a few minutes the snapping gets faster and faster. Therefore, the daydreaming is shorter and shorter. You must fabricate new daydreams quicker and quicker. If this process were represented by a line for daydreaming and a dot for finger-snapping, it would look approximately like this:

——————————————— .
——————————————— .
————————————— .——— .
————————— .————————— .
————— .
— .————————————————— .
——————————— .————— .—— .
—————— .—— .——— .————— .
——————————— .
————————— .———— .—— .
——— .——— .—— .—— .—— .—— .
———— .——— .—— .—— .—— .

At the beginning, the length of the daydream is varied; toward the end, the daydreaming time becomes shorter and shorter. Change the subject of your daydream at every snap.

Watch your body respond to these mental acrobatics: notice tensions produced by the command to change your daydream. These tensions may be very revealing.

Do these high mental acrobatics for a few days: your mind, freeing itself of worn-out circular daydreaming, will be eager to imagine creatively.

To worry about having failed to accomplish certain tasks and projects in the past is like worrying about the countless number of sturgeon eggs that did not hatch—instead of enjoying your caviar.

"HAD YOU KNOWN HOW TO SUFFER . . ."

In one of the Gnostic Books—The Apocryphal Acts of John —there is a passage which is connected with the Sacred Dance that Christ performed with his disciples. It reads:

"Had you known how to suffer, you would have been able not to suffer. Learn to suffer, and you shall be able not to suffer."

In this recipe we attempt to apply Christ's advice. We are concerned here with the most intense emotional (not physical) suffering. To some persons this may seem a cruel recipe, yet it is effective and necessary.

The essence of this recipe is to suffer willingly and consciously at a certain predetermined time—in acute cases, one hour out of the twenty-four—to do this intensive suffering *then* and to refuse to suffer during the other twenty-three hours. During that allotted hour, we suffer to the extreme. And how difficult this is! Suffering will attempt to elude us during that hour, but how powerfully it will try to intrude during the other twenty-three! We have to say to suffering: "I have a rendezvous with you tomorrow at seven—not now." Still, during that hour, no matter how determined and firm you are, something will try to distract you from *suffering* here and now, and during the rest of

the day distract you from *living* here and now. The sweet
memories of the past will rush to the doors of your heart,
like a hungry crowd clamoring for attention—remember
that look   remember those words   remember that infinite embrace   remember the brilliant day when love and
intelligence and beauty were all there at once! You cannot
forget the timeless totality of being that shouts at you,
imperiously demanding your attention. How can you deny
attention to the loveliest, most precious part of your life?

Remember . . .

Remember . . .

Remember . . .

The past will keep on and on, pounding at all the gates
of your soul, pressing at each pore of your skin—and you
must deny its dictatorial demand, for that is the past. Your
memories are ghosts, and you are not a ghost living in a
ghostly land. You are a human being living here, between
heaven and earth.

We cannot avoid suffering. It is as much a part of life as
is joy. We cannot obliterate it, no matter how hard we try.

We are told in physics that water is uncompressible. Try
to press or push water. Its volume will remain exactly the
same, only the shape changes. The same thing happens
with suffering: Try to forget and suppress it and the shape
will change, but not its essence or its power. Impeach its
spontaneous expression and it will express itself in some
other way—probably affecting that part of the bodymind
which is most vulnerable and weak. Much of our suffering
comes from an insistent voice from the past still wanting
to be heard because it was not fully listened to at the right
time. So it persecutes us throughout life, demanding the
full attention that was not given when the suffering began.

"Had you known how to suffer . . ." What does Christ

mean? It seems to us, he means that when there is suffering
(and we speak mainly of *major emotional* suffering), we
must accept it fully in its unreasonable, inhuman cruelty.
We must suffer with all of our being, completely awake,
completely aware that there is no rationalizing, no forgetting, no avoiding. Only by giving in to it completely, by
even stimulating an expression of this suffering, will we
be able "not to suffer" the same sorrow again and again.
In so many ways, Christ insists that we be here now, even
when the here-now is so painful that we try to escape by
forgetting it. We push it down, and there it stays for years
and years like an imprisoned starving rat, gnawing at the
inner lining of our gut, sucking all the sweet juices of our
being, so that sometimes it is difficult for the sufferer to
cry, impossible to feel sensual or sexual satisfaction, or
sometimes impossible to love.

Many of us have had in our lives one or more tragic
events, that is, events that changed the quality of our life.
The emotion contained in that event may be constantly
present, just below the level of consciousness. Like a record,
it plays continuously inside us until we cease to hear it with
our superficial ears, although our whole organism is per-
meated night and day with its emotional vibration. In some
cases the event is forgotten by our *fact* memory, but not by
our *emotional* memory, which influences our vital body
functions. Many undiagnosable pains, aches, malaises, de-
pressions, exhaustions, etc., originate that way. When a
major pain is not fully lived at the time it happens, it
might remain in the tension of certain muscles; in our
emotional attitude toward life; in the words we say; in the
relationships we choose—or don't choose. All of this might
happen without our conscious knowledge.

In other cases, we are completely conscious of this long-endured sorrow and, as with anything which stays with us long enough, an unwholesome attachment develops, as in a marriage whose partners stay together only to torment one another. Our grief might even give us some minor satisfaction, such as attracting the attention and indulgence of other people.

Sometimes suffering might fill a need for more intense living. In Christian and Jewish tradition, suffering is considered a nobler feeling than joy. We are stuck in lamentation. This is a tragic predicament, because it allows anything to evoke our pain; any little event, any objectively insignificant fact, can be felt as an all-important sorrow. Sometimes our voice acquires the plaintive quality of that first "Oh, no!" with which we met the original pain, and we continue to salute new events in the same tone.

There are four main ways to deal with suffering.

The first way is suppression—the attempt to forget it, to smile even if it hurts. But the smile is a grimace—we cannot ignore what is there.

The second way is living the pain, but living it only halfway. A draining identification with suffering begins and it may color every other aspect of our life. Then the pain sticks with us as too big a bite will stick in the throat, refusing to go down or to come up. The popular phrase "I cannot swallow that" is accurate both physically and emotionally.

The third way is the way that Christ advises: living our grief fully, consciously and intensely for the very purpose of becoming free from it; going into it to enable us to get out of it. Having given it full expression, we begin to detach ourselves from suffering. It still exists, but it is no longer so deeply interfused with our being, so closely identified with our life. When it is no longer darkly shut within, we make a space between suffering and ourselves.

Having liberated our energies from the grip of *mechanical* suffering, we can then deal with what is left of it in the fourth and highest way: transform it into useful and beautiful actions, through artistic and humanistic endeavors.

To shatter the paralyzing grip of suffering takes an act of courage; it requires awareness and an Attentive Will. The following directions are intended to teach us how to suffer so we don't *have* to suffer.

> Choose one hour a day which you will put aside for this recipe. (Choose, if possible, the same time every day.) During this hour disengage the telephone, put a "do not disturb" sign on the door and take all precautions possible to prevent interruptions. This is your time, and yours alone.
>
> Sit very straight on a straight chair.
>
> Do not read, or move around.
>
> Do nothing but: concentrate on your pain in any way which intensifies it—play emotion-stirring music, think of anything that makes your pain more vivid, dive into it as into water. Something in you may attempt every possible frolic to distract you from this courageous decision to suffer here and now, willingly and fully. Beware of this something, and when it tries to take you away from your suffering, come back to it NOW. This hour, and not the other twenty-three, is the hour for suffering.
>
> Let the pain express itself in any way it will—let your tears flow, scream, moan, speak—do anything that can bring your suffering out, be it posturing, drawing, writing, talking.
>
> This effort to control pain might have been very valuable, even essential, the first few times you tried it; then the attempt became automatic, fixed, frozen. It involved not

only a mental decision, but a corresponding and completely physical contraction, a restriction requiring tremendous exertion. No wonder one is so often exhausted. Retrace the physical effort connected to your repressed pain. Often, as has been medically and empirically shown by Dr. Ida Rolf, the emotional pain is quite dissolved, but its physical expression is there—a reality as hard as rock. So feel this effort. If you don't feel it, ask yourself: "Which part of my body would I tense or contract if I made an effort to control and hide a strong painful feeling?" This question will quite certainly bring you a physical answer. If, by a slim chance, it should not, then use your imagination. Make up a story in which you describe a man or woman controlling his emotion, and what happens to his body at the time. As you write or visualize this story, observe your bodily reaction. You will find your answer there. Whatever happens, keep on this step a long time. We use vast amounts of the energy needed for other pursuits to control and to push down the valuable energy of emotions we don't want to acknowledge. What energy is left for living, creating, enjoying, if so much is spent to control it? This situation is almost as mad as our national defense, which deprives all of us of precious energy in order to build so vast a defense that we have enough homicidal weapons to kill each human being on this planet FORTY-NINE TIMES!! Let us not duplicate the same insanity in our personal lives!

In all probability, one or many symptoms may emerge as you experience this recipe. These may be pinpointed and acute, or diffuse, preconscious feelings. Here are a few of the myriad symptoms that might emerge: butterflies in the stomach, pain in the neck, discomfort in the digestive system, tension in some muscle of legs, arms, shoulders, difficulty in breathing, contracted sphincters, difficulty in swallowing, dry mouth, dizziness, locked jaws, grinding teeth, tension in the eyes, twitching in the face or other part of the body, palpitations and other sensations in the heart, sudden pain in places we are not usually conscious of. If you have any physical disturbance or problem, this step might reveal to you its origin, and, more important, might start a healing process. When any one of these or a similar symptom appears, go with it—even if it is unpleasant. Don't repress it—NOT AGAIN! This is the hour you have decided to give to suffering so that you are free of suffering for the remaining twenty-three. Let the symptom guide you to the best solution. Express this pain in any way you choose: write, dance, draw, howl like a wounded animal or sing like a nightingale, write poetry or pound your fists (or pound the bed with a tennis racket, which is extremely effective), contract your whole body and hold your breath as long as you can, then let everything go! We will list some of the innumerable ways of achieving release on page 248. Choose one or invent your own.

If you need a little more time, take it; but it is better to train yourself to do this suffering at the time and for the length of time predetermined.

If when you are finished there is emotion left over, tell yourself that tomorrow at the same hour there will be total freedom to plunge willingly into the pain again.

After you have been practicing this recipe a while, you will feel that grief is not your very essence. After you have opened all the doors on which grief was banging desperately to enter, you will finally be able to tell pain that it is not a permanent resident in your house but only a temporary guest.

Variation:

Experience this recipe in the "Between Heaven and Earth" position (see the next recipe) for the length of a record specially chosen for its meaning to you.

When a jestful imp turns green lights into red just when you are about to cross the street, turn the joke on him by transforming your frustration into an invigorating action: rhythmically contract and release your anal and/or vaginal sphincters while whistling or singing a lively march or dance.

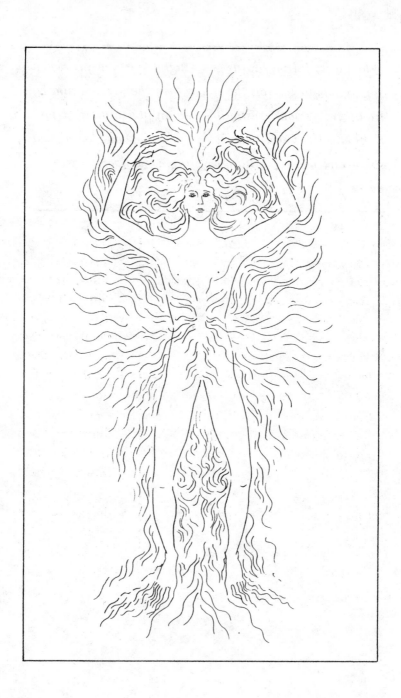

BETWEEN HEAVEN AND EARTH

This recipe simply consists of assuming the position in the illustration. It represents our situation between heaven and earth. The first time I gave a seminar with this title I wondered what image to use to illustrate our situation so that each person would experience it with his whole being. Only an hour before the seminar this image leaped into my mind—so obvious! By holding the position just five minutes, I experienced how sensations and ideas flowed in, through and out of me. Since then numerous other people and I have had varied and sometimes profound experiences while holding this position for differing periods of time; reactions including trembling, sweating, laughing, singing and crying have taken place. Sometimes undulating tremors fluttering from the feet all the way up to the crown of the head have resulted in great and unforeseen releases of tension. The reports of people who have experienced the "Between Heaven and Earth" position are considerably diverse:

I found my roots.

I could be anywhere.

I found my will power and it is immense.

I wanted to shout HURRAY! I was so joyful.

It was very painful at first—then a deep relief swept over me, and I cried.

It was easy—I felt as though I were hanging from the sky.

I discovered my body.

Afterwards I experienced the deepest sleep.

The first five minutes were painful; then I felt a flow of energy.

Initially, it was very difficult, I wanted to stop. Then it changed and was amazing.

So much happened to my body, as though it were fixing itself; I felt that new paths of circulation were opening.

Why holding this particular position for a certain length of time brings so many varied and strong reactions, I do not know. There are probably as many explanations as there are theories. What I do know is that when this recipe is done correctly, it usually yields a benefit greatly out of proportion to the time invested in it. When we assume this position we seem to expand toward high heaven and deep earth, receiving and metabolizing energies of which we are ordinarily unaware.

Look at the illustration and imagine that the lines of the arms and legs, as well as the vertical channel traversing the head and trunk, go on and on—reaching, expanding all the way to infinity. When you take this position, experience a sense of extending yourself to infinity—of becoming an empty channel filled with the energies of heaven and earth. The energy flowing through fingers and toes is usually felt first; then an exchange and a mixing of energy is strongly felt through the trunk, from above and below.

Directions:

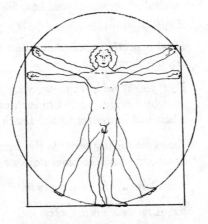

This figure is a rendition of the well-known drawing by Leonardo da Vinci. We show it here to point out that it is considerably different from the "Between Heaven and Earth" position . . .

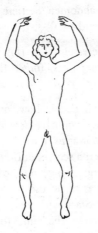

. . . which looks like this.

In the beginning, it is better to do this in front of a mirror in order to check the following:

> Body is completely perpendicular to the earth. Imagine a straight rod, uniting heaven and earth, entering at the top of your head and exiting at the crotch.

> Head is gently poised; don't push it or pull it in any direction.

> Feet are as wide apart as your hips, pointing straight forward, parallel to each other. Keep the whole foot in contact with the earth.

> Knees are slightly bent. As you become more proficient, the bend becomes deeper and deeper.

> Arms form a soft curve above head.

> Palms face each other a few inches apart. Fingers are open and softly bent.

> Shoulders are relaxed. (Do not elevate shoulders when you raise arms.)

> Hips, abdomen, derrière are not pushed forward or backward.

All details are essential to this position. When you have checked these points, forget the mirror and close your eyes.

Before starting, decide how long you want to hold this position. When you have decided, go through with it and don't bring your arms down or change the position of legs or feet for even a second during the time you have set for yourself. If you change position, start all over from the beginning. It is of no use to do this recipe for less than ten minutes. Start with ten minutes for a week, then gradually increase the time to half an hour or more. Generally the benefits increase in proportion to the time devoted to the recipe.

It is effective and much more significant to do this recipe while listening to music. Choose something that is meaningful and moving for you.

Because this is a private experience, I recommend listening through earphones. Moreover, the sounds that reach you directly through the ears vibrate through your bones. This is helpful in releasing subtle and hidden tension, and if the music is appropriate, it enhances basic body rhythm. However, do not turn the volume loud enough to burst your eardrums. This has happened to some people too greedy for "experience."

Involuntary motion of the body, such as trembling, quaking, shivering, quivering, jerking, oscillatory and undulatory movement, might occur. Do not try to control it. It is beneficial. You can always stop these movements at will. Let these reactions take place in your body and observe them without judgment. They indicate that some adjustment is taking place. Let it happen. It is your deep vegetative soul in the process of making you well. Do not interfere with its workings.

Similar unexpected reactions may take place on the emotional level; crying, laughing, sensations of strength, weakness or pain may alternate in an amazingly short span of chronological time. While doing this recipe your biological and emotional time might differ from chronological time.

It takes about a month of daily practice to become aware of this recipe's remarkable power. At the end of a month you will easily be able to keep this position for at least the length of an LP record and experience surprising and beneficial reactions. The choice of the music is very significant to the experience. Conclude with the following movement, which should be done very slowly with your eyes closed. Feeling what happens inside your joints as you move:

Lower your arms in a wide, slow, circular movement while your hands turn to face the earth. (If you are a student of Tai Chi Chuan, conclude with the closing movement of this practice.)

Simultaneously lift your right foot, bring it near the left and straighten knees.

Relax hands and arms; let them hang.

When you are standing straight, arms hanging relaxed, remain motionless, eyes closed, feeling the changes that have taken place inside your body.

Stand still for a minute or as long as you like: this is a precious moment of heightened inner awareness.

Variation One:

Do this recipe with your eyes open in front of a mirror. Keep a steady look at a small point between your eyebrows.

Variation Two:

After you are well acquainted with this recipe, you might experience it with someone who is also familiar with it.

It is advisable to choose someone who has had more or less the same amount of experience with this recipe.

Agree with each other on the length of uninterrupted time to be spent on this recipe. This is essential and must be decided in advance.

If you do this recipe with music, agree on the choice.

Take the position and stand facing each other about three feet apart.

Look at each other steadily throughout the time allotted;

focus your gaze at a small point between your partner's eyebrows.

As suggested when doing this alone, do not stop any physical or emotional reaction—let it happen.

This recipe experienced with a partner in the manner described may be a highly significant, even poignant event.

The difference between what is natural *and what is* habitual *is substantial but very subtle: to detect it we need patience and an alert objectivity. A bad habit—poor posture, daydreaming, thinking in circles, tense voice or jerky movements—seems natural after many years. The purpose of re-education and higher disciplines is to inhibit the* habitual *and permit the* natural.

YOUR SIGNATURE, PLEASE

To do this recipe you need a long roll of shelf paper and a good many pens or pencils.

Sign your name in as many different ways as possible.

Sign it as if you were sad, gay, peaceful, agitated, furious, rejected, enlightened.

Sign your name as you remember and/or imagine you signed it when you first learned to write, as you signed it in all different periods of your life.

Sign it as if it were for the last time.

Sign it as an indweller of heaven.

Sign it as a denizen of hell.

Sign your name as you did on the most important documents of your life (marriage, divorce or other contract).

As you do this be aware of the difference in the muscular activity of your body for each signature. Your muscles are partly directed by your conscious will and imagination, and more so by your subconscious activities.

When you have finished writing your name in all possible ways, put the paper away. Look at it again after a few hours or the next day. Examine your signature and find similarities and differences. See if there is a constant factor in some letters.

Grapho-Therapeutics: Pen and Pencil Therapy, by Paul de Sainte Colombe, teaches how to know oneself by an analysis of handwriting and, if one desires, how to improve oneself by consciously changing subconscious drives through the act of writing. You might not have studied grapho-therapeutics yet, but by first *feeling* your muscles as you write your signatures, and by then studying the signatures, you will understand more deeply your many-splendored personality.

Here are the directions for a variation of "Your Signature, Please":

> Lie down in total comfort and privacy and see that you will not be disturbed for one hour. Close your eyes. Now, with an all-reaching imaginary pen, write your signature on:
>
> a menacing cloud
>
> the bottom of the ocean
>
> the vast sands of an undiscovered desert
>
> the boundless blue sky
>
> the rich earth
>
> your favorite star
>
> an agitated sea
>
> the space between two distant planets

Write your signature between heaven and earth.

Write your signature on timeless space.

Write your signature with:

> letters of fire
>
> letters of blood
>
> letters of tears
>
> letters of gold

Write your signature:

> with musical incense
>
> with evanescent letters
>
> violet scented
>
> tenderly singing

End this recipe with an affirmation of your extraordinary destiny:
> connect heaven and earth with your signature

Variation Two:

Do this recipe with any name or nickname you might have had during your lifetime.

Who is the wisest wizard: the one who makes extraordinary things seem easy and accessible, or the one who makes easy and accessible things seem difficult and inaccessible?

YES–NO–YES

The first YES in this recipe represents the fundamental drive of life; the NO represents the obstacles to that drive; the second YES the overcoming of those obstacles. It is obvious that we have said YES to life; otherwise we would not be alive today. To be convinced of this, we need only consider the prodigious trip that one particular sperm, among billions of others, must make to reach its destination. Comparatively, it is a longer and more dangerous trip than going to the moon. The tiny sperm has its own "Van Allen belts" to go through before reaching its distant home. That invisible sperm must indeed be a YES creature to triumphantly embed itself in the ovum.

Then we have the long period of gestation to complete. This is not, as is often thought, a time of uninterrupted organic pleasure. The fetus is one with the mother and is affected by any upset in her being. The fetus has no self-image, no feeling of individuality. It exists and grows only in union with the mother. Few mothers have an idyllic pregnancy; this period often seems to compound problems rather than solve them. Every situation is felt by the fetus. A person who has come from what is called a *good womb* will be able to go through life's difficulties without serious mental breakdown. A person whose pre-natal existence was unwelcome, is likely to repeat in life that same pattern of rejection. Unless this pattern is brought to consciousness and dissolved, the individual will need considerable determination to overcome inhib-iting feelings. We must not forget, however, that since we are here now, alive, even the most painful womb did not prevent us from saying YES to life.

The major event of our life, birth, is comparable in its magnitude only to death. In the ideal situation, where both mother and father are healthy, loving, and have been preparing together for the natural outcome of an act of love, birth is surely one of the most exalting events. But how often does this idyllic state occur? In our modern society, birth is handled mechanically, sometimes after the failure to abort, and the new creature is likely to be sur-rounded by fear, confusion and loneliness. As though the shock of being separated from the inner part of the mother's body were not enough, the new creature is often separated from the warmth of human touch which is at that time the very river of life. And what of the slap with which he is generally greeted on entering the world? There is generally little respect in the treatment of the newborn, especially in large institutions where he is handled as though he were a thing—unfeeling and mind-less, needing only to be filled with food as a car is filled with gasoline. This initial treatment is, in all probability, responsible for the basic sense of aloneness from which we later suffer. But we survive that too. Miraculously, we con-tinue to say YES to life. Fortunately, this negligent attitude toward the newborn is changing, thanks partly to Dr. Frederick Leboyer's book, *Birth without Violence*.* This

---

* *Birth without Violence*, Frederick Leboyer. Alfred A. Knopf, 1975.

work reveals the preternatural beauty of a child born in silence and peace, among people aware of his defenseless nobility.

We go then through infancy and childhood depending on our parents, the supreme giants, for food, shelter and love. Without them we would die, and how often these ignorant giants say NO, and again NO, and again NO! We had already picked up the feeling of negation through unpleasant and dangerous changes of chemistry, and vibrations during the prenatal and birth period. But now, in childhood, we are picking up the very word NO. And one day, usually around the age of two, we discover that we can, just as the giant does, say NO. What an intoxicating feeling of power to say NO, just as the giants do! And then not just to say NO, but to be NO! with our whole tiny, powerful body which can emit noises totally disproportionate to its size. How can we ever relinquish this godlike power? In many of us negation becomes automatic or, even worse, rationalized.

This blind power is the NO in our recipe. I am not speaking about the many times and situations in life in which we must legitimately say NO. I refer to the innumerable NO's we say automatically and blindly, because of an unfriendly, negative feeling we acquired long ago. Few individuals remember when this negative feeling was acquired. Many of us have just a general, unpleasant sensation about the origin of our negativeness. This recipe is designed to get rid of those self-defeating NO's which our surroundings, our parents and our educators have inflicted upon us. Sometimes this negation has legitimate reason, but frequently it is the result of automatic conditioning.

The most difficult NO's to dispel are those that, having been imposed on us early in life and, consequently, having been deeply embedded in our subconscious, we feel are part of ourselves. Opinions and decisions which direct our life often originate in unconscious negative feelings. If we want to recapture our freshness and freedom and be able to take decisions with a clear heart and mind we must get rid of any automatic negativity. We are speaking not merely of verbal negation, but of attitudes which involve our whole being. How often our body says NO in spite of our vocal expression to the contrary! Our NO may be expressed in a negation of health; or in self-righteous political stances; or in generally spending more time and energy blasting hell than praising God.

At this point you may feel that there are so many NO's in our system and our environment (Realize! You have survived them all!) that you might conclude you can do very little about it, and reject the following recipes.

If you say NO to these recipes, there is every likelihood they were designed for you.

Following are six recipes which comprise "YES–NO–YES."

The *first* is to let go of any possible negation that existed before and at the time of conception.

The *second* is to erase the NO's which we felt during the nine months of uterine life.

The *third* recipe is needed to dispel all those NO's filled with the fear and pain inflicted during birth.

The *fourth* and *fifth* recipes are devoted to the first two years of your life.

The *sixth* recipe can be applied to any year of your life.

General directions:

"*I will get rid of all unnecessary and damaging NO's.*" This may seem a naïve direction, but without this initial personal commitment limited results can be expected. This conscious self-programming is basic to erasing unconscious programming originated by our environment and accepted by our organism.

Set aside one hour, preferably at the same time every day. Be sure you will not be disturbed or interrupted in any way.

Close your eyes but don't relax. A listening, non-judging attitude is essential.

To fully experience these recipes, we must accept both our imagination and our memory, for here they will melt together. See memory and imagination as two rivulets joining in one large river. It is impossible to distinguish which part of the water came from which rivulet, and so it often is with memory and imagination. These two merge into one. It would take a lot of energy to find which drop belongs to which rivulet! For this recipe let us unite the words "memory" and "imagination" into one: "memo-imagine."

We don't know how far back our memory goes. Workers in this field report memories not only of past lives, but also phylogenetic memories of primitive states of being. This recipe is equally beneficial for those who believe in its logic and realism and for those who feel certain states of being cannot be re-experienced—that is why we have made that word "memo-imagine." Some of us will use more, or entirely, the memory; others, the imagination.

This recipe is equally efficient whether you are convinced that it is the imagination, or the memory, or both, guiding you—as long as you approach it with an open state of mind.

1. Preconception and Explosion

Lie down in a quiet room. You have not yet been conceived. What originates birth? The desires of your parents? Your own desires, unfinished relationships or deeds?

Were you a consciousness before you were born?

Whatever the initial cause, go now to the point in time before your conception. According to Dr. Motoyuki Hayashi the egg life is between twelve and twenty-four hours and must be penetrated by the sperm within that limited time span.* You are now going to experience that period of time—however, chronological time has very little to do with your biological memory of this event, and the intensity of hours of experience is relived in minutes. It is the quality of the experience that counts.

A man and a woman have made love. Five hundred million sperm cells are now racing toward their destination— the oviduct in which the egg is traveling on its way to the uterine castle. Like the fabled sleeping beauty, her unmanifested energies inviting the princely touch which will awaken her to consciousness and love, the egg is waiting for the piercing touch of the sperm which will begin the miracle of individuation. Without it, the egg will recede

* *1975 Edition Nature/Science Annual*, **Time-Life Books**.

into anonymity with countless other perishable cells. The racing legions of sperm are surging, swirling, dashing through rivers of sweet elixirs and deadly chemicals. Like salmon, they must swim upstream against the fluid currents of the oviduct in order to reach the egg. One out of the five hundred million will avoid, surmount, destroy and use all the obstacles encountered on his dramatic voyage. Only one will individuate, some giving up the race, some easing the way for those who have greater mobility and a more compelling impulse toward immortality. Soon the competition will become keener, more desperate. This is serious business wherein the winner, possessing and possessed by the egg, will become a godlike creature. The others will end as an anonymous crowd.

You feel both the tranquil and dynamic waiting of the egg and the compelling race, the fundamental need of the sperm.

You feel the sperm wiggling upstream, daring and overcoming all obstacles. It has been reported to me personally, by many people, that the moment of conception is often experienced by the fully conscious individual as an explosion of lights, as spectacular as the most splendid fireworks. I don't know how you will experience your conception, but don't be surprised if it feels and looks like a burst of illuminated energy to match the most effulgent sunburst you have ever witnessed.

It is very beautiful to feel the duality, the differentiation of egg and sperm, and then the explosive "becoming one." This relinquishing of two separate identities for a fusion into one—a dissolution of subject and object—is found at every turn of our spiraling evolution, from two simple chemicals in the primordial soup to the mystical union with God. It is the giving up of the limited self for emergence into vaster consciousness. It may be the most primitive unicellular organism or the highest product of evolution: at whatever level, this convergence is always an uplifting sensation of liberation, of newness. I don't know of any instance where conception is felt by the conceived as a negation. I know of numerous instances where it is relived by persons (not under hypnosis or drugs) as a triumphantly divine YES, as a "bliss beyond bliss, all other joys transcending."

2. In the Making: Womb-Life

Lie on the bed or on the floor. You are in your mother's womb. At this time you have no words or voice. You feel and react with the whole of your little body.

As you lie there, move and feel as you memo-imagine to have done as an unborn creature.

Take any position that comes easily to you, but find a natural, rather than habitual, posture.

Get into your body which as yet has no voice. You might enjoy a feeling of liquid bliss. However, this period is not always smooth and comfortable. Emotional, physical, mechanical disturbances may affect your mother and her environment. These are the NO's we have been discussing, representing discomfort and pain, rejection and the fear of it. Let these NO's out in every possible way other than your voice. Don't be concerned with the medical exactitude of how a fetus moves. We know that it moves and kicks. Move in any way that feels good to you, in any way that might relieve any possible negation imposed upon you, an unborn baby.

In this period of memo-imagining your uterine life, you may notice a deep, possibly startling, change in your breathing. When we are in the womb our lungs are not functioning yet and we breathe through that miraculous organ, the placenta. So, in reliving that period of your life, your breathing might at times become very quiet and almost unnoticeable, as though you were breathing and taking oxygen through your skin. Although we are no longer breathing through the placenta, the breathing that occurs in reliving the prenatal period is at times almost imperceptible, and has a strange and deeply peaceful quality. Let it be! You will enjoy it immensely.

Do this recipe as long as you can and stop only when you feel that you have exhausted for the time being the emotion it has stirred.

When you have finished, take a cold shower or dash ice water on your face. Jump up and down one hundred times, arms wide open, loosening your wrists, and letting your hands flop up and down. As you do this say, shout, sing: YES! YES! YES!

3. *Birth*

Now let us get rid of all those discomforts, pains, fears, those NO's imposed upon us during birth. The birth trauma is considered by some schools of psychology to be the basic and most important influence on our feelings about life and death. Being born can be a dangerous ordeal; the sensation of being suffocated is frightening. Some researchers believe that much of our fear of death has its origin in the precarious hour of birth. It is this pain and fear which, for the sake of clarity, we express in this recipe as NO.

It is advisable to do this recipe with the assistance of a supporting partner. Make a free hour or two for yourself.

> In a quiet room, on the floor, involve all of your body and mind in memo-imagining that you are coming into this world.

> Your partner will not interfere by expressing his own feelings or ideas; he will simply be there, attentive and supportive. Silence is preferable but sometimes a few generalized words, such as "good," "all is well," "fine," are more helpful than any specific direction. Above all, it is with his attitude that the supporting partner can help you.

It is impossible to give specific directions since births vary widely in the length and pain of labor, the methods used by doctors and nurses to help the baby emerge, the position of the baby in the womb, and whether it is a natural, anesthetic, or Caesarean birth.

Re-experiencing one's own birth might be either a pleasant or a painful and dramatic experience or both. Be prepared for anything, and whatever happens, keep in mind that you have gone through this birth victoriously or you would not be here. Also keep in mind that the purpose of reliving your birth is to be here more fully and to win your freedom from the negative part of that experience. As long as this negation remains unconscious, it is likely to trick us into attitudes, opinions, and actions which repeatedly reinforce the vicious circle of negation. If you are unable to directly contact the birth trauma, then combine your knowledge of it with your imagination, letting imagination lead you.

Your partner must be very careful to see that you end this experience feeling well and in the present time.

When it is completed, stand up, eyes open, hands open, legs open, your entire body stretched as wide and as tall as possible.

Be aware of breathing.

As you inhale, feel the rush of cosmic energy entering you.

As you exhale, say in any tone, any rhythm or manner you like, YES! YES! YES! Let it be a murmur or a shout, YES, YES, YES—timidly or boldly, YES, YES, YES—intensely or lightly, YES, YES, YES—repeat it for at least fifteen minutes.

It is desirable that your partner participate in this. Find the lightest, gayest, liveliest piece of music and, dancing with your partner, sing, "I am alive and well," or any song which expresses the feeling of buoyancy.

4. *Zero to One*

You are a little baby now, between zero and one year old. If those great big awkward giants, unaware and powerful, could know how many times they make you uncomfortable and unhappy! They don't know that the slightest wrinkle in the diaper in the wrong place feels like a big rock under your tender skin. They forget what a shocking loss the refusal of mother's breast can be. Maybe you were one of those babies who suffered from the erroneous dictums of several decades ago. It was then considered right to let you cry for the good of your lungs; to make you wait for your food for the good of your character; and to let you lie alone in your crib and deprive you of the warmth of an embrace so that you would learn early to support loneliness and separation. In fact, the tragic structure of self-rejection and loneliness is based on early isolation and on untimely disciplinary methods. What does so young an infant do to fight this early indoctrination and to show his rejection of it?

> *Be that child now. At this age, you do not walk, but you can crawl; you do not speak, but you can let your voice express many meanings; you can lie on your tummy and*

do all kinds of fancy movements, or lie on your back and kick in many unique ways.

With the assistance of your supporting partner or alone, express all your NO's as long as there are any left in you, and until you feel exhausted and free. Do this longer than you think you can.

When you are really finished, deep, rewarding sleep is beneficial. Even a short sleep will give you a complete rest. Wake up in the here-now. Take a cold shower, eat something fresh and raw. Enjoy saying YES to each bite you take.

5. *One to Two*

Now, by virtue of your own inner rhythm, which has nothing to do with the giants' chronological time, you are moving toward, and you reach, the powerful age of two. Everything in you is changing. You are taking in and absorbing not only your food, but much more. What is your tiny, yet immense, organism absorbing? What, out of the boundless possibilities of the outer universe, do the giants around you offer? *They offer themselves*—the food, the bath, the clothes, even the toys the giants give you, are an extension of themselves. Because the giants are often oppressed with their own problems, you get these troubles along with your food, your bath and your toys.

Some giants, either naturally or by disciplined consideration, learn to temporarily put aside their troubles when they are with a child. Unfortunately, this rarely happens. In our society there are many laws and regulations on buying and selling, on taxes and their exemptions. We are confronted with time-consuming procedures at every turn. Permits are required even to install a dishwasher in our home—but no question is ever asked about whether a person or a couple is fit for parenthood. If prospective natural parents were put through the same severe procedures required for adoptive parenthood, a great step would be made toward a more enlightened society. At present it is not so. The fact is that you are getting to be two years old, and it is very likely that you have already absorbed a multitude of NO's. We cannot dwell on, much less judge, which of these NO's are useful and even necessary to your survival, and which are damaging; which NO's were inspired by love and wisdom, and which were an extension of the giants' limitation, pain or aberration.

You are going to free yourself from those NO's that are no good to you NOW. Your voice is strong. You are two years old and you have learned the magic word which has confronted you many times. You can stop a household with that word—NO! You can say it to the food, to the bathroom, to sleeping. What power you have acquired! Why relinquish it? Why, indeed, unless a more powerful NO is imposed over yours? Is your life going to be a battle between negations?

The period from conception to the age of two is paramount in laying the foundation for our attitudes throughout life. These attitudes can be changed during one's life —at times in a moment of revolutionary insight, at other times through a slow growth process, and generally through both. The age of two, when we acquire the power of negation, not only by bodily expression, but by the very word NO, is a particularly important turning point. The danger is that we may become trapped in a negative power which may then dominate us for the rest of our life. When we are its unconscious slaves, the power of negation is like a strong narcotic that puts us to sleep— sometimes until the final sleep. Strong negation at life's beginning steals large portions of our intelligence, our capacity to love, our good will. It steals the best part of life. A negative programming is as mechanical as a record which plays the same tune, whether played at the Equator or the North Pole, whether listened to or ignored. Most of us have, to some extent, automatic NO's in unaware corners of our sleeping selves. Sometimes these NO's emerge, evoked suddenly by an outer stimulus or a special state of our health.

Directions for "One to Two":

> You are reaching the age of two. Place yourself where you cannot be heard, and where you cannot hurt yourself or anyone else.
>
> Lie on the floor, and memo-imagine how, as a creature two years old, you sometimes fearfully accept, sometimes desperately fight, against any intrusion on your budding individuality.
>
> Kick, scream, shout, throw a tantrum, run on four legs, or on three, or two. Let any basic animal feelings express themselves in any way they will. From time immemorial, these instincts and feelings have been with you. Our general word for them is survival, and it is survival (real or imagined) that makes you reject other people's NO and makes you shout your own. It is the affirmation of your being.
>
> End this recipe by taking an hour-long walk during which you direct your attention to the smallest detail: but focus only on those details which are at a height of between five and seven feet. If you walk in the country notice the smallest spots on vegetation and flying insects or birds—whatever is between five and seven from the ground. Similarly, if you walk in the city notice details in people's faces and ornaments; look at their hair and whatever is a little above their head.

It is desirable to have a cooperative partner who will assist you in this recipe—and whom you will later assist.

6. *From Two to Now*

The recipes you have just completed take you to the age of two. From now on we will not give specific recipes for a specific year. Devote at least one session of the following recipe to each year of your life.

You remember certain years more clearly. They have more NO's and YES's. There are blocks of years which seem to have completely slipped away from you. Sometimes those years were happy years—sometimes so painful that you have "forgotten" them. While doing this recipe you may be surprised by the sudden appearance of forgotten and important YES's and NO's, events and feelings which unexpectedly emerge from a particular year you previously thought insignificant.

The year or period which marks a new activity or event usually holds more material to review and relive. Similarly, the year or years which mark the passage from infancy to childhood, childhood to adolescence, etc., are particularly memorable.

It seems certain that there is a part of our being which has recorded everything that ever happened to us. This information is frequently available.

When you have decided to give this recipe one hour for each year of your life, follow these directions:

Set aside one hour, preferably at the same time every day. Be sure you will not be disturbed or interrupted in any way.

For the first fifteen minutes or so of this hour, sit straight in a straight chair or take the "Between Heaven and Earth" position.

Concentrating on the year selected, let memories and feelings emerge.

During the next half hour, or for as long as necessary, express what emerges.

Express the NO's and the YES's.

Express them by:
dancing or writing
shouting or talking
painting
exercising
playing an instrument
changing the placement of the furniture in your room
digging in the garden
running
swimming

But, attention! Don't let the activity distract you. Keep focusing on the fact that this present activity is a means to express the NO's and YES's of that year of your life.

Each recipe of this YES–NO–YES series ends in the same way: with YES! Unless you feel ready to express a total YES, with all of your bodymind—a full surrender to life—the session is not finished.

However, according to how you developed the recipe, there are several ways to bring about that final YES. Choose the one most appropriate for you. Give yourself fifteen minutes to:

Listen to serene music.

Meditate on a flower.

Be in the "Between Heaven and Earth" position.

Lie with legs and arms wide open on the floor (or better, on the ground). From heaven and earth a multitude of luminous YES's are converging into you, target of loving energy.

Perform a YES action toward yourself or another person.

Make silence within.

Bake YES cookies for everybody, as Ginny, a friend of mine, used to do.

Variation:

For many of us, experiencing YES–NO–YES for each year of life is the best method. Other persons do not clearly connect events and feelings with a specific year. The following method may be preferable.

Read the general directions (page 83). Do not think of a specific year of your life. Remember instead one of the events or feelings in the following list (devoting at least one whole session to each entry):

First day in kindergarten
     day in school
     toothache
     illness
     hint of sex
     conflict about sex
     awareness of money
     awareness of not being liked or loved
     night of honeymoon

time you realized many things are not right
time you realized you are not the center of the world

First time you didn't like your parents
   felt rejected
   felt shy
   felt alone
   felt ugly
   felt unintelligent
   felt you didn't like yourself
   did something for which you felt guilty

Any of these events or feelings will most likely bring similar ones to consciousness. Events are important but the feeling is "the thing."

First express the feeling.

When you feel free of it, reflect on how it has influenced your life decisions and attitudes.

Do you agree with them?

Part Two

Just as a circle cannot be interrupted at any point and still be a circle, so the circling bodymind energy, if misdirected, will distort the function of the organism. Let us be especially aware of this circling of energy in the recipes in "Nutrition, Transformer of Consciousness."

NUTRITION, TRANSFORMER OF CONSCIOUSNESS

Imagine that you are a tourist guide. Your assignment today is to introduce to the American life style a newly married couple just arrived from an unindustrialized country. You are scheduled to take this couple to visit three places: a supermarket, a bookstore and a drugstore.

At the entrance of the supermarket the smooth-rolling carriage fascinates the bride, who probably visualizes several babies in it. You explain the carriage's use. "But it is so big!" she exclaims. Now is your opportunity to introduce your client to the psychological persuasion of our Western (and wasteful) world: "The carriage can contain such large quantities of food and still look empty," you say, "and it rolls effortlessly even with fifty pounds of food. That makes it easy for us to buy more than we really plan to."

You are not sure whether this is understood. Better start touring: there will be no necessity to explain since the superb display speaks for itself. The overall view of the supermarket elicits delight and wonder in the visitors. "How can there be so much food? And everyone taking it out so matter-of-factly? And what is this? And what is that?"

A good guide, you take them to each counter. The variety of vegetables and fruits is astounding. There are even many types of milk from which to choose. "How many kinds of mammals are there in America?" the couple wonders. Once in a while, they recognize with pleasure an item which is like one they use at home. Then you show them the yards and yards of cans containing every kind of food. You tell them that the cans may have been on the shelves for several years, and still we eat their contents. The variety of frozen food is even more astonishing; the communication is facilitated by the pictures on the packages.

Then you walk between two parallel shelves. On the longer shelf, cats and dogs are pictured on the packages: on the shorter shelf, babies. The visitors are surprised that in this country we eat cats and dogs . . . but why the baby pictures? You are fairly successful in explaining about the baby food, but explaining the cats and dogs proves harder. "All those cans and boxes are not full *of* dogs and cats," you explain. "They are special food *for* dogs and cats." "Special food *for* dogs and cats?" the two keep repeating. After a discussion with his bride and trying to show his sophisticated understanding, the man asks, "And the special food for jaguars and snakes—where is that?"

At the end of the visit your couple is exhausted and ready to eat. You tell them that all the food is at their disposal but not just now. "We must keep our schedule and visit the bookshop." Specifically you are going to visit the department on nutrition and cooking. You explain that all these books deal with the food they just saw. The two look at each other and smile politely: relating all that food to all these books is really hard. To clarify this issue, you read the titles: *How to Eat and Be Thin, How to Eat and Not Be Fat, How to Eat When*

You Are Upset, How to Eat When You Don't Want to Eat, How to Eat When You Are Born in January, in February, etc. Then you show them the millions of recipes with the colorful photos and directions on how to mix foods together: a mixture of ten, fifteen ingredients in one dish to be eaten with another dish which is equally complicated. It boggles the imagination of the young couple, who are by now wondering whether with all this food in print they will ever get something to eat.

But it is not quite time yet. Now you are to show them a giant drugstore. You stop by one of those long counters where hundreds of medicaments are displayed. "Pretty packages," the young lady says. "What is inside?" You explain: "These are medicines to help you digest the food you saw—to assimilate it and eliminate it, to supplement it in case it is not enough. These pills give you an appetite, and these take it away, and these are to make you feel good even if you eat too much . . . and these . . ."

About to faint, the two young people fall into each other's arms: love seems to be the only solution.

Although we have gradually been habituated to the avalanche of overabundance, we too are often bewildered about the flood of advice on food and nutrition. The variety of schools, methods, beliefs regarding diets is a new phenomenon. It is, however, a logical consequence of the variety of food made available by our technology. There is now at our disposal food grown anywhere in the world at any season of the year, whereas until fifty years ago we ate mostly seasonal and local food. The disturbances in our organism have similarly multiplied. So has the scientific knowledge of our functions, and remedies for our dysfunctions. Nutrition is a subject involving an increasing number of disciplines: finance and medicine, agriculture and chemistry, anthropology and psychology, politics and humanism, technology and mysticism. Don't fear! We have neither the space nor the knowledge to delve deeply into these subjects. It is, however, amusing to think, when scrambling our breakfast eggs, how many forces have converged to create the possibility and the desire for us to do so. And it is encouraging to think that some of the best cooks in the world, as well as some very well-nourished people, never consider the complications involving food and nutrition.

The three processes of nutrition—destruction of food, conversion into energy and elimination—are all-embracing because they represent the very cycle of life. What we put into our body is only part of nutrition. The question is: *how much and what do we assimilate?* A museum guard may spend years among the greatest paintings in the world, yet he may never *really* see and absorb a single one of these works of art that people from all over the world come to admire. Similarly, no matter how well we eat, we are nourished only by those foods which we can convert into ourselves. No matter how glowing the food's chemical analysis looks, if what we ingest is not assimilated, it remains in our system as surplus, and we are both undernourished and intoxicated. As Sir William Osler stated: "Only a small percent of what we eat nourishes us: the balance goes to waste and loss of energy."*

Only when our body, imagination and will collaborate in assimilating what we eat do we derive vitality from it. In food and nutrition the interrelation of these three basic elements is very powerful. Our body will not convert

* *Food Is Your Best Medicine,* Henry G. Bieler, M.D. Random House 1965.

into healthy energy something that we eat against both our will and our imagination. If our imagination suggests that a specific food will make us feel good, it may do so to a degree, even when our will falters. But no good can be expected to come from eating something which both imagination and will do not accept as good. It seems to me that the nutritional value of the food we eat should be considered as three points of an equilateral triangle:

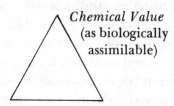

Chemical Value
(as biologically
   assimilable)

Quantity, Quality, Combi-
nation (as suited to individual temperament and
purpose of eater)

Pleasure
(taste, smell, appearance;
where eaten and with
whom eaten)

Such a balanced triangle leads to the balance of another beneficial triangle:

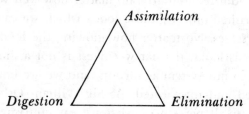

Assimilation

Digestion   *Elimination*

A harmonious bodymind state follows.

When studying nutrition two facts are evident:

the adaptability of human beings

the individuality of human beings

Our adaptability is illustrated by the fact that there are human beings in good health in different parts of the world which may not have a single item of food in common.

The individuality of human beings in regard to nutrition is best illustrated by the research of Roger Williams, Ph.D. He impressively shows the enormous difference between individuals considered "normal" and leading similar life styles. Our organs, chemistry, blood and gastric juices have more striking individual differences than our faces. "If normal facial features varied as much as gastric juices do, some of our noses would be about the size of a navy bean while others would be the size of a twenty-pound watermelon."*

Twelve of the drawings below are of *real* stomachs. The one on the top is a "textbook" stomach. The others, all from normal subjects, neither look alike nor operate alike.

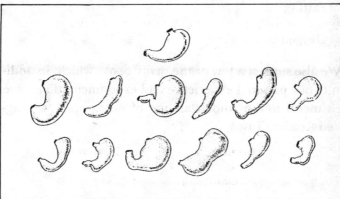

After Anson, B. J.: *An Atlas of Human Anatomy.* W. B. Saunders Co., 1950. Reprinted with permission.

---

* *You Are Extraordinary*, Roger Williams. Random House, 1967.

The same is true of our hearts, livers, spleens, of our nerve endings, our blood, our glands, etc. All are directly or indirectly involved with nutrition. Given these extraordinary differences, it is not surprising that schools of nutrition often conflict with each other.

It is not within the scope of this discussion to evaluate the different schools of nutrition. We will instead make a few comments on these salient points:

Personal Relationship with Food

Buying Food: Quality and Quantity

The Preparation of Food

Vibrations

Diet and Supplements

Fasting

Oxygen

We also suggest a few of the many books which, in addition to our personal experience and experimentation, have been useful to our understanding of nutrition. (See Suggested Reading List.)

Personal Relationship with Food

Our choice of food is to some extent dictated by circumstances: our manner of eating is extremely personal. Do we taste food with our own taste buds or those of mother, father, lover or the ideal man or woman we have seen eating on TV? Do we eat it because we are hungry? Or because we are angry or frustrated? Or because it is time to eat?

When we eat a morsel are we eating it here and now —or at a time years ago? Or are we thinking of the next bite? Are we aware of the act of chewing? Of absorbing part of the food through the tongue and finally swallowing? How far can we follow the food? Our gastrointestinal tract is between twenty-five and forty feet long. How long is our awareness?

When we eat, do we feel the taste or the texture? Or the person who prepared it? Or the one who is eating with us? Do we eat the smell, or the color? It is amusing in this context that pet-food manufacturers make dog morsels to look like marbleized meat, whitish and reddish, as though the dog could see colors! Good psychologists, pet-food manufacturers know that dog owners like marbleized meat for themselves and consequently buy for their dogs what stimulates their own liking.

Eating is survival—physical, psychological and emotional. Obviously we have to eat to survive physically. Psychologically we often eat because we are a part of a group, and wish to be like other people. We sit in a restaurant with an acquaintance; we invite and are invited to share food with friends. Often families see each other only around the table. Emotional eating is a well-known phenomenon. Probably the greatest part of eating is not done for physical survival, but to fill an emotional emptiness. It may be a sexual need, or an avoidance of unwanted duty, or distraction from present frustration, boredom, restlessness.

A child's hunger may provide a good excuse for delaying his homework. Some of the child is left in us; we often eat to postpone doing something, or thinking, or facing a problem or an emotion. Furthermore, since eating is, up to a point, a legitimate need, we don't feel the need to masquerade or hide it.

> For two or three minutes during every meal observe yourself with the purpose of seeing your relationship with food. You may be surprised at how farfetched your discovery is.

Buying Food

QUALITY

In 1970 the Food and Drug Administration reported that our food contains at least 10,000 chemicals (food additives and their residues).* These chemicals are used to preserve, cook, freeze, tenderize, spice, color and package food so that it will last as long as possible. Similar procedures were used in Egypt five thousand years ago to mummify the important dead, preserving their bodies in good condition tor as long as possible. When buying food, the best general rule is to buy only those things which would last just a few days if left at room temperature. Some exceptions are milk, butter, oil, milk products and eggs.

Buying food can be enjoyable. It is rather arresting to

* "The components of food resulting from technology are usually considered as 'food additives and residues.' Some compounds are added to foods directly; others are produced as a result of various forms of processing; some occur as residues from seed, soil or crop treatment; some are residues of drugs or other additives fed to animals; and some come from migration of packaging materials into foods. Estimates of the number of those compounds vary, but according to one authority, 10,000 is probably a conservative estimate." Leo Friedman, Ph.D., *FDA Papers,* March 1970.

think, as we do our marketing: that peach is going to become me—and also that cadaverous beef is soon going to be me!

Try this little recipe: when you shop speak to yourself, inserting your name in the blank.

_____, *those strawberries are going to be you!*
_____, *those cherries, that fig are going to be different parts of your body;* _____, *that canned fish is going to be you;* _____, *that dead duck is going to be you;* _____, *that artichoke, that banana, that cheese, all are going to help your heart to beat, your brain to think, your eyes to see;*
_____, *that apple, that lettuce, that genuine bread are influencing your chemistry, your moods, and therefore your relationship with people—therefore your life.*

If this realization is present in your mind when you shop for, or touch, or cook food, you might awaken your vegetative soul or body wisdom to know what to choose, when and how much to eat.

To understand and feel the connection between the state of our being and the food we eat is to understand and feel our connection with our environment. Eating an orange and squeezing its juice with our tongue, if done with awareness, can put us in touch with the sun, the earth, rivers.

QUANTITY

Excess in drinking is about as bad as excess in eating.
—Hippocrates

A sad consequence of our society's use of affluence are the numerous clinics, dietitians, books, gyms, spas, clubs and M.D.'s specializing in bariatrics—all concerned with helping millions of people to lose excess weight. Except in a small percentage of cases, excess weight is due to ingesting more food than the body is capable of using. Being "overfed and undernourished" is more prevalent in America than anywhere else.

The overweight person *shows* that he eats too much; but most of us overeat to some extent. If we don't show it, it is because we are lucky enough to have a more balanced metabolism. If we would eat only to fulfill our physiological need, the intake of food, assuming it is of high quality, could probably be cut at least one-third. There are people who live on a fraction of what most of us eat and still feel good and strong. I am not referring to mystics living in the desert or on secluded peaks, for in such cases the quality and quantity of food is naturally changed and diminished by the life style and environment. I am speaking about people who work fifteen or sixteen hours a day and live on a small amount of food, not as a deprivation, but because they find it convenient and pleasurable. These persons have the capacity to extract from food nutritional values unwritten in the tables of chemical analysis. This capacity may be the result of:

> Economic necessity, which awakened body wisdom to choose and utilize the proper quality and amount of foods

An awareness of the difference between real and false hunger

A state of consciousness which permits the eater to extract energy from food and air in a way unknown to most of us. *Prana* is a form of energy which people trained in yoga learn to absorb; others do the same through a natural gift

A more efficient system of respiration, yielding more oxygen to the cells and so increasing assimilation

Total trust in a Higher Power to guide the body

Most people who by choice fare on very little do so with a different spirit than those who gorge themselves. Maybe the high energy-absorbers are no longer living defensively or aggressively, but are aware of the wonder of food, and approach it with a certain respect. This attitude is not present in those of us who eat as though consuming food were an act of defense, attack or revenge.

Although there are many theories regarding the causes of longevity, it is generally agreed that people who eat less live longer.

Is it possible that the number of people dying prematurely because of eating too much is comparable to the number dying because of eating too little?

The Preparation of Food

The preparation of food is an important part of nutrition.

One may buy the best food and destroy its flavor and value by cooking it carelessly. It is best to eat raw or lightly steamed food whenever possible.

The mood of the cook is an important factor in cooking, for his vibration becomes part of the food itself.

If cooking is not a pleasure, let each member of the family prepare his own food. That is why I have devised the Cooking Meta Toy described in the following section. With the Meta Toy and basic fresh foods (fruits and vegetables, cheeses, eggs, cereals) excellence and variety can be had without the necessity of cooking when unwell or unwilling.

The greatest challenge in cooking is to combine nutrition and taste in the same dish. If a dish is full of nutrition and unpalatable, its nutritional value will be greatly diminished. Just the idea that *what tastes bad is good for you* is unnourishing! On the other hand, taste alone cannot nourish us for long.

Vibrations

We eat vibrations with our food. No matter how nutritious the food is, if it is eaten in an atmosphere of conflict—irritation, rage, worry, fear or hate—part of that food will be polluted by those emotions which are converted into various illnesses: heartburn, indigestion, migraine, ulcer, cancer, etc. The subtle alchemic change from psyche to soma, from emotion to body, is not a change in essence, but only a change in the vibratory rate. One musical scale gives us infinite modulation, and similarly infinite are the modulations from emotional to physical states and vice versa. We each have our own way of modulating the basic scale of conversion from body to mind to body. A meal eaten in anger may bring indigestion to one person, migraine to another, sore throat to someone else. This is why we have emphasized so often the need to express consciously and harmlessly, in fact beneficially, any inharmonious feelings. In this way, the alchemic transmutation is done mindfully toward life, instead of mindlessly against it.

Even the best planned nutrition can fail unless the vibrations while eating are good. Sometimes it is difficult to really taste the food if one speaks, so eating in silence seems a good way to eat deeply and well. But this applies

only if the silence is a symbol of harmony and security between the eaters, rather than an indication of resentfully
accepted authority, or repressed thoughts and feelings
ready to explode. Eating with the sound of music is, to me
at least, too full of emotions. Even pleasant emotions may
have too strong a repercussion on the digestive system.

American restaurants are rigorously controlled by hy-
gienic authorities. Much untouched food is thrown into
the garbage merely because it has gone from the kitchen
to the dining table. (The general waste of food in this
country would be considered a crime in a more enlightened society.) What about some psychological hygiene?
Feelings of hostility, anger and resentment are far more
toxic than any contamination that might be contracted by
a piece of bread going from one room to another! The
atmosphere in most restaurants in great cities has everything but purity and sincerity. It is no wonder that so
many Americans suffer from all kinds of digestive difficulties. I'm not speaking here of the artificiality of food but
of the attitudes of the people who handle food. The cook
should be made to realize the importance of his attitude
toward preparing food, and so should those who serve it.
Due to the packaging of precooked food, the restaurant
cook's role has been diminished, as have his pride and zest
in the art of cooking.

I like those small *trattorias* in Italy where the cook looks
out from the kitchen to see how the first bite of his dish is
received. I rarely go to a restaurant and usually, unless a
friend cooks for me, I enjoy preparing a simple meal.

Family meals sometimes turn into a battlefield; but
even fighting armies have a truce at especially holy times,
such as Christmas. All family meals could be given similar
consideration. Each member of a family could agree on a

suspension of hostilities during their meals together—or eat alone. Emotional storms sometimes clear the air and usher in better relationships, but the digestive tract is strictly connected with our emotions and to ingest food and toxic emotions simultaneously is the surest way to invite illness. Obviously we don't suggest a *suppression* of feelings—only a *suspension*. Moreover, after eating we feel more solid, our blood sugar is stabilized, and we can express our position more eloquently.

Diet and Supplements

What is a good diet for me? This question cannot be answered until some of the following questions are answered:

Where do you live?
How old are you?
What kind of job do you have?
Is your sexual life satisfactory?
How do you feel toward yourself?
With whom do you eat?
What do you dream?
What is your last thought at night?
Are you in love?
What is your first thought in the morning?
Do you have children?
Is your sense of smell a keen guide, or do you hardly notice it?
Is the intensity of your emotional feeling markedly different before and after a meal?
Do you breathe consciously sometimes?
Do you have a totally satisfactory relationship with one or more persons?
Do you meditate?
Are you now living in a condition physically, psychologically or emotionally stressful?

Your answers to these and other questions, coordinated with your genetic heritage and chemical analysis, are basic to your choice of diet and food supplements. If your air, water and food are free from those 10,000 additives mentioned previously, and if your emotional life is equally unpolluted, then your nutrition is probably excellent; taking supplements would be superfluous and wasteful. If you are not one of the few fortunates who enjoy such unpolluted life, the choice of supplements must be made in relation to the quality and quantity of the food you eat; whether you take supplements for a specific weakness or for general prevention; whether you want to enhance your capacity to be active or your capacity to be tranquil. In leisure time we need fewer nutrients than when under stress. Psychological upsets, surgery, noise, shocks, drugs, infections, etc., greatly increase our need for supplementation. But it is impossible to establish a general rule. The late Adelle Davis, a most thorough researcher, states, "It seems to me there is only one way to determine the quantity of those vitamins which will make you feel your best: Find your own dosage. Learn how to vary the amounts from day to day depending upon your body structure, the quantity and type of food you eat, the strain of your work and exercise, the stresses you are under, and the amount of liquid you drink."*

With diet and supplements, as with everything else, *you are the measure of all things.* By developing an acute awareness you will increase your knowledge of your needs. Sometimes the effect of what we eat or drink is immediately perceived. This applies to alcohol or coffee, both of which are such strong drugs that their effect is obvious. It takes subtler perception to feel the effect of a

* *Let's Eat Right to Keep Fit,* Adelle Davis. Harcourt Brace Jovanovich, 1970.

leaf of lettuce! There is a good variety of information available. Although no one has been able to create an apple by combining all its nutrients as listed in the tables of food analysis, such tables are important and helpful. Consult them but do not wed them!

Experience and attention will help you to differentiate between your real needs and your habit or addiction. The minimum daily requirements established by the government, considered far too low by nutritionists, are oriented toward avoiding serious diseases, like scurvy and pellagra, rather than toward achieving a high level of health. Moreover, since our environment is continuously and unhealthily modified, we must now select a *defensive* nutrition to balance the additives and pollutants which enter our body-mind without our choice or knowledge. Throughout his development man has had to fight for his life against wild beasts, excessive heat or cold and shortage of food. These enemies were known and "out there." Now we are in the unprecedented position of having an enemy inextricably interwoven with our means of survival: air, water, food. What we breathe, drink and eat keeps us alive but it also contains elements pitted *against* our lives! Moreover, the enemy has achieved its power in a time infinitely shorter than needed by our evolutionary protective capacity to develop natural defenses. Higher dosages of supplements may be a *temporary* solution. However, the fact that solving problems with means familiar to us is at times impossible may be a warning and inspiration to find other, hopefully higher, more creative means. Einstein said it, years ago: *"The world that we have made as a result of the level of thinking we have done thus far creates problems that we cannot solve at the same level as the level we created them at."*

More and more the necessity to step higher faces us in the most unforeseen situations. Whether we are coping with problems of food or relationships, breathing or loneliness, this necessity forces us to realize how interwoven seemingly distant subjects are in reality—and how inescapably their solution depends on our level of consciousness.

Fasting

It is not paradoxical to discuss fasting in connection with nutrition. One of several reasons why even top nutrition may fail to yield expected results is that our body is overworked by the unsuccessful attempt to digest and eliminate. Fasting gives the body the possibility of clearing itself. There are numerous records of cures by fasting, collected since the beginning of civilization.

A fascinating ancient document on fasting comes to us from Christ in the book *The Essene Gospel of Peace.** I know of no writing, whether medical or mystical, which communicates so precisely and poetically the oneness of our physiological and spiritual processes. This book's detailed directions for fasting and clear explanations for the

* *The Essene Gospel of Peace*, known also as *The Essene Gospel of John*, was discovered in Aramaic in the library of the Vatican and in Ancient Slavonic in the Library of the Habsburgs in Vienna (now the Austrian government's State Library) by Edmond Bordeaux Szekely, who compared, edited and translated both manuscripts. It was published in English in England and the United States in 1937 and has been since translated into German, French, Spanish and fifteen other languages. Available from the Academy of Creative Living, 3085 Reynard Way, San Diego, Calif. 92103.

need to fast are today as timely as they were two thousand years ago. It is one of my pleasures to give *The Essene Gospel of Peace* to friends. Those who "assimilate" this short book derive more benefit from it than from long treatises and learned lectures.

While fasting, the body takes a vacation from its work of digesting and absorbing food to concentrate its forces on eliminating waste matter. Sometimes the walls of the intestines are encrusted with toxic residue, which impedes optimum absorption of nutrients, and generates an excessive need for food. When cleaning is accomplished we need less food because we assimilate better.

One of several reasons why fasting is so often miraculous is that it depends on a deep decision by the person fasting. It is an act of will toward better health and higher consciousness that no one else can do for us. It is a deeper commitment than that given to other treatment in which doctors, nurses, pharmacists and others are involved.

Think how many people have been involved in the process of making a pill! First the pharmacologists put together the proper ingredients in the right dosage. Then the drug firms have board meetings on the financial feasibility of the project. Then follow experiments on animals and humans, as well as permission from the government. At this point your pill is a pile of paper on a Washington desk. Then the pill is accepted and manufactured. An army of public relations experts and salesmen go to work making the pill acceptable to doctors and the public. They succeed. Your doctor gives you a slip of paper which you take to the druggist; he requests some money, and finally! the pill is in your hand. You only have to swallow it. Fasting is a simpler, less expensive procedure but it depends almost completely on you—FASTING IS ALL YOURS!

The basic condition for fasting is that it be undertaken voluntarily and under expert direction. Here are a few general suggestions.

There are different degrees of fasting: fasting on vegetable juices is different from fasting on fruit juices or on water. The choice of type and length of fast depends on your situation. Five days of fasting is usually considered a good length for the first one.

It is better to fast away from your usual environment, especially if it is in the city and involves other people keeping their regular eating habits. Solitude and/or a supportive environment are important.

For the period of fasting choose an interesting project or a subject on which you want to be enlightened (children, painting, money, death, garbage, flowers, joy . . .). As your fast progresses the subject you choose will, in all probability, bring to mind many subjects you thought were totally unrelated.

When you fast be sure to move quite energetically without exhausting yourself. Do not remain static or you will impair one of the main functions of fasting, which is elimination. Exercise and walk three or four hours a day if you wish to avoid very unpleasant aches and pains. There is sometimes a so-called "healing crisis" at about the third day, which marks the point after which fasting becomes pleasurable. Generally no trace of hunger remains after the third or fourth day.

You might want to sleep several times during the day —possibly for short periods—so try to be free of appointments during the fasting period.

Before undertaking a fast read on the subject or consult an expert.

From the time we are born, eating is a strong structure

in our daily life. When that structure is shaken many psychological and physiological functions are shaken too. That is one of the many reasons why a fast is often revelatory. Again and again miraculous cures have been reported as the result of fasting. A recent triumph has been the recovery of hopeless schizophrenics. After years of mental illness and after every other *possible* treatment had been tried, a thirty-day water fast with three hours a day of physical exercise succeeded. This treatment was conducted at the Moscow Psychiatric Institute by Dr. Uri Nikolayev and his staff. It was repeated in New York with the same results by Dr. Allan Cott, M.D., of the Huxley Institute for Biosocial Research.* As the physiological toxins are cleared away, so are their mental and emotional counterparts.

Records of fasts, sometimes lifelong, can be found in the history of mystics. One of the most extraordinary is Theresa Neumann, the Swiss mystic, who for thirty-five years lived without food or water. She could not swallow at all. The sacramental wafer which she took every morning slowly dissolved in her mouth. For thirty-five years the function of elimination was absent. Her weight remained more or less the same and her health good. She underwent long and strict controls and examinations by medical doctors. The phenomenon remains unexplained by current methodology. During the Third Reich the Bavarian village of Konnersreuth, where Theresa lived, was put on food ration. It was officially recognized that she did not eat, so no food stamps were given to her. She received instead an extra ration of soap to wash the sheets stained with the blood of the stigmata which appeared on her hands every Friday.

* "Controlled Fasting Treatment for Schizophrenia," Allan Cott. *The Journal of Orthomolecular Psychiatry*, Vol. 3, Number 4. 2135 Albert St., Regina, Saskatchewan, Canada.

Maybe at our next evolutionary twirl we too will have learned to extract energy directly from the sun and air. This would eliminate the complicated and time-consuming process of extracting it by growing food, eating, absorbing, etc. Animals in their natural state spend most of their time providing for food. We have evolved enough to spend less time on food and nutrition. In the future our attention may be increasingly focused on different levels of being and on new, unforeseen pleasures. Consequently we may be able to nourish and enjoy ourselves in a way less cumbersome and primitive than that which we are now using. A fast gave me a glimpse of that future possibility. Obviously, in our present situation, we are not equipped to live on air only, nor inclined to give up the pleasure of eating.

Oxygen

And the key to the whole thing is oxygen.
—Kenneth H. Cooper
  *Aerobics**

The following principle is the most important factor in nutrition; it is hard to believe that it is so seldom mentioned in books on the subject. The fact is that NOT UNTIL IT COMBINES WITH OXYGEN IS OUR FOOD CONVERTED INTO ENERGY!

By a miraculous series of transformations, what we eat is broken down into carbon and hydrogen fuel. But: "Not until they are within the cell . . . do the carbon and hydrogen fuels meet the oxygen. This, the final transaction, is the *burning process,* the oxygenation of our food that *provides us with our energy.* Biologists mindful *that this is the vital result of our breathing* refer to the cell's oxidation activity as respiration."**

In his famous book *Aerobics,* Kenneth H. Cooper, M.D.,

---

* *Aerobics,* Kenneth H. Cooper. M. Evans & Co., 1968.
** *Man and His Body,* Benjamin S. Miller and Ruth Goody. Simon & Schuster, 1960.

puts it this way: "In its simplest terms, any activity requires energy. The body produces energy by burning foodstuffs. The burning agent is oxygen. Even down at Cape Kennedy, the rocket boosters carry fuel and an oxidizer to burn it for energy. Once they leave the atmosphere they run out of natural oxygen so they have to carry it with them. Aircraft, which stay within the atmosphere, use the oxygen in the air to burn their fuel. *In the body, the fuel is food and the flame is oxygen.*"

It is obvious, then, that the best nutrition comes to nothing unless it combines with oxygen—for it is this union that "provides us with our energy."

In the recipe "Breathe More, Eat Less, Love More" I report the findings of Dr. Otto Warburg, twice Nobel prize laureate: cancer cells die in an environment sufficiently saturated with oxygen.*

From the chart below you will see another representation of the importance of oxygenation in our body: it is the vital system which declines the fastest in aging.

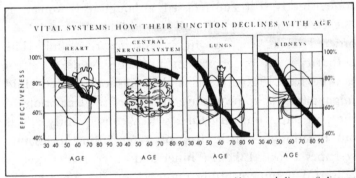

Newsweek-Fenga & Freyer

* *The Prime Cause and Prevention of Cancer*, Otto Warburg. Translated by Dean Burke. National Cancer Institute, Bethesda, Md., 1969. Available from International Association of Cancer Victims and Friends, Inc., 5525 El Cajon Boulevard, San Diego, Calif. 92115.

At fifty we have reduced our oxygen intake to a third of what it was at thirty. This reduction of oxygen affects every other system in the body. It is important to ask: is this reduction irreversible? The answer is a strong NO. Breathing is voluntary as well as an involuntary function. We can breathe more if we decide to do so. Why is our breathing so reduced by the time we are fifty? In part, this reduction is due to physiological causes over which we have limited control, but there are other causes over which we do have control: the basic one is unawareness in the use of our body. Unless we are vigilant, by the age of fifty we have acquired a great number of habits, and *habits murder awareness.*

Why do we breathe less?

All of our emotions influence our breathing. Not only our present emotions, but those of the past as well. We may feel healed from past traumas, but our body still bears their imprints. Women often carry their shoulders as they did at the time their breasts began to swell: the adolescent is still embarrassed although the woman is not. Or the man may still pull his shoulders back as he was ordered to do years ago by an authoritative adult. The authority is no longer present, but the shoulders are still pulling back. Sexual fears and repressions in the child might affect the spine of the adult. All of these emotions of the past affect our structure, which consequently affects our breathing. A little drop of water falling incessantly reshapes a rock. Likewise inner and outer events exert a powerful if imperceptible influence on the more or less 20,000 breaths we take every day. Twenty years later we find that our intake of oxygen is cut by a third. To compensate we eat more and better, we take more vitamins and supplements. It all helps, but the best remedy is to directly restore our breathing to its highest possible efficiency.

Not only emotions of the past affect our breathing. Notice for yourself: when doing difficult tasks, or in a tense situation, or when sad and listless, don't you breathe more shallowly?

> To get more oxygen, we must make a place for it. Only by emptying our lungs can we make this place and we achieve this by exhaling completely. When we exhale incompletely, which is most of the time, we retain stale air in our lungs and bronchial tubes. The precious space we need for oxygen is filled with carbon dioxide. Our purpose is to make space for fresh air. So exhale—press with your hand underneath the ribs and the abdomen until you are sure all the old air is out. When you are empty, you can almost massage your inner vital organs—liver, spleen, intestines—while remaining empty a little longer than it seems possible. Don't worry about inhaling! Nature will do that for you. Air will rush in as a liberating angel and you will realize the privilege of breathing as you have never realized it before. This will only happen if you stay empty a little longer than you think possible. Do this before getting up in the morning and again when in bed at night. Repeat this breathing three times during the day, especially before and after demanding work or disturbing situations. By increasing the oxygen in our system this breathing will help to reverse the processes of degeneration of the cells, thus stimulating a general rejuvenation.

More and more we must defend ourselves from the outer robbers of oxygen: smoking or breathing other people's smoke, car exhaust, polluted air in crowded rooms or in traffic. In polluted environments the scarcity of oxygen is further reduced by shallow breathing. Instinctively we breathe deeper when we are out in the fresh air of the country: but how much of our life do we spend in the country?

In conclusion: Oxygen starvation affects our ability to see, smell, hear, taste; it hampers our sexual enjoyment, our ability to think, to move, to love. In other words, *it diminishes us.* It is a creeping scourge fed by our un-awareness—a murderous intruder, silently stealing our life at every moment.

Change this picture of gloom, EXHALE NOW!

Here are means to increase respiration other than the basic fact of breathing:

Complete nutrition and proper use of nutritional supplements. Vitamin E is especially important. Without it the body's need for oxygen is tremendously increased.* Also important are the active group of respiratory enzymes (iron, riboflavin, nicotinamide, pantothenic acid and other nutrients).**

Meditation. Breathing is almost always improved even in those types of meditation that are not directly concerned with breathing.

Exercise. Without motion the best nutrition is useless. If we don't move, the nourishment doesn't either. Food energy might indeed turn against us if it becomes static. Most doctors agree that the victims of heart attacks often eat too heavily in relation to their sedentary life—"sitting addiction," Aldous called it. From breakfast sitting—to car sitting—to office sitting—to restaurant—to office—to

* *Let's Eat Right to Keep Fit,* Adelle Davis.
** *The Prime Cause and Prevention of Cancer,* Otto Warburg.

dinner—to TV sitting! Who can compute the millions of heart-attack victims who would be alive and well today had they not become car addicts?

Today, more than ever before, the choice of exercise is fascinating and vast. In addition to swimming, bicycling, running and walking, we have Tai Chi Chuan, yoga, dervish dancing, Aikido—all types of exercise and dancing coming to us from different cultures, ages and places. Certain exercises are more beneficial to the muscles, others to circulation, others to oxygenation. They are all beneficial to our bodymind.

The system of aerobics (meaning "with oxygen") is especially designed to increase oxygenation; it is both preventive and curative. Over the years, the remarkable and far-reaching results of aerobics have made medical history.

Yogic breathing. The highest, most sophisticated art and science of breathing has been developed by the Eastern yogis for five thousand years. If you are interested in developing the art of breathing and its far-reaching effect upon your bodymind, find a teacher of Hatha Yoga. He will show you how to increase oxygenation and to be receptive to *prana,* or life force.

Olfactory awareness. The sense of smell has been with us longer than our other senses. It is also the deepest sense, partly unconscious and strictly connected with breathing. We cannot smell without breathing although often we breathe without realizing that we smell. I can see now Aldous's amused smile when he quoted a theory postulating that man thinks he chooses his woman because she is beautiful, charming and wise but in fact he chooses her because he likes the way she smells!

Give your nose a leading part in your life. It is one of our greatest leaders, whether we realize it or not

A book's smell is important: I hope this one smells good!

Before buying food smell it. People, animals, objects— all have distinctive fragrances which greatly influence our relationship to them. Do you remember those touching words of a Negro spiritual: "Sweet-smelling Jesus . . ."? The churches have always known the value of respiration. Through incense, singing, chanting and movement most religious rituals increase oxygen intake. Allah—Alleluia— Hare Krishna—Rama: these words represent different creeds, dogmas and rituals, but when those sacred names are sung and chanted our cells do not speculate about dogma. They only profit by receiving more oxygen.

A charming illustration of this is an Indian story Ram Dass told me:

There was a great sinner who went to a great teacher and asked him how he could purify himself of his sins. "Chant Rama [an Indian name for God] a thousand times a day," advised the great teacher. The sinner went to a solitary mountain and chanted and chanted. But, in spite of his good will, he made a mistake and chanted Mara instead of Rama.

After years of chanting, he went back to the great teacher, who immediately realized that the man was now pure. "Did you sing the sacred name?" the teacher asked.

"Yes, Great One!" the ex-sinner answered. "For ten years every single day and thousands of times I have chanted MARA MARA MARA."

The teacher burst into laughter that shook the mountains. As his laughter, like a pebble in a lake, vibrated farther and wider into the cosmos, the great teacher took the ex-sinner into his arms. "Your will to good has saved you," he said. "Even though you

chanted millions of times Mara   Mara   Mara, the
name of the devil!"

Will to good above all—and (may I be allowed to add)
oxygen!

My decision to be a vegetarian was one of those fortunate instances where reason and instinct danced together. Suddenly I couldn't face another piece of cadaver. It was an instinctual command. My reason agreed with it because:

Animals are given hormones to grow faster than nature had planned.

I don't want to eat hormones indiscriminately.

At the time of slaughtering, which generally is not conducted in humanitarian ways, rage and fear pervade the beast's body.

I don't want to eat rage and fear.

After the animals are killed, the meat is treated with many additives for color, preservation, texture. Some of these additives are known to be injurious to health, even carcinogenic according to an increasing number of researchers.

I don't want to eat carcinogens.

The decision to exclude meat from your diet must come from within. For me, the above are sound reasons for making that decision, but they may not be for you. This is Alan Watts's thought on the subject: With his irresistible loving wit, he said that it would be all right to give care and love to a cow, not forcing its growth but allowing it to develop in green pastures at its natural rhythm and in good company. Then, having provided it with a good life, one could also provide a painless death with the salute: "I love you so much that I am going to eat you!" This privileged cow would be transformed into a being on a higher evolutionary level and the whole process would be a natural and loving one.

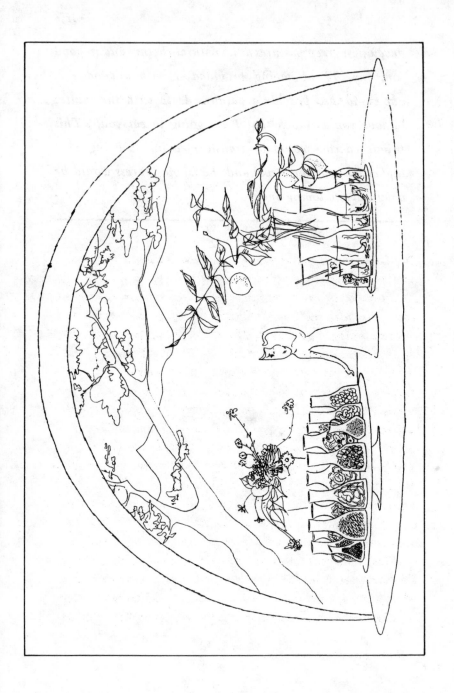

THE COOKING META TOY

My basic recipe for cooking is a *meta* recipe: a recipe to make your own cooking recipes.

If someone were to wake up in one of our large American cities after a hundred years of sleep, he would be overwhelmingly surprised. The physical and psychological changes in our style of living would, in all probability, astound him as much as the shock and wonder of our technology. As Norman Corwin puts it: "In the old days we tended to find things out for ourselves, we experimented, we read, discussed, weighed, measured, *thought* for ourselves. Today we take somebody's word for almost everything; we are manipulated by the most persuasive advertiser, the biggest display, the smoothest and most fatherly men, the administration handout, the sharpest slogan to buy this shampoo or that candidate, this car or that explanation, to swallow this price hike or that priority."*

This trend to think less and obey more is applicable to our cooking. Considering the number of cookbooks, plus the thousands of recipes offered daily by the press and the media, one would think that food is an element foreign to

* *Westways* magazine, April 1974.

us, and that even to warm up some water we need direction. There is value in being given new ideas and a knowledge of foods unfamiliar to us, as well as a taste of distant countries and different cultures. I can enjoy Alice Toklas's cookbook, even if I do not make those rich and sophisticated dishes. Such a cooking style gives a glimpse into an intellectual group with the keenest taste buds, and into a style of life which has almost vanished. But it is a pity to abdicate the pleasure of "doing our own thing" to follow rules of measuring and weighing and timing. This tendency to follow what we are made to think are important rules seems to be stronger in America than in Europe.

Our old friend, helper and artist cook, Marie Le Put, who is French, was teaching me how to broil a chicken. The whole procedure was very simple. She only insisted that, after it was cooked, I must leave the chicken in the oven before serving it. I asked why. Patiently, she answered, "Madame, because it must rest before being served." I became curious about the length of the rest period. "How long should it rest?" She looked a little surprised. "Well, you see," she said, "it depends on how it feels."

My sister, visiting me from Italy, made some delightful sauces; I asked her to write them down for me. The last line of each recipe reads, "Taste it, and add what is necessary." And that is the way I suggest to end *all* recipes.

Here I offer you the "Cooking Meta Toy" recipe, meaning a recipe with which to make your own recipes using a Cooking Meta Toy. As with a Tinker Toy you can build a big palace or a little boat, so with the Cooking Meta Toy you can make recipes for different times of the day and different people or meals. I will show you later how to build your own Cooking Meta Toy and make your own recipes on the spur of the moment. I don't particularly recommend rushing, but when time is short it is advantageous to be quickly creative; it is better than eating food packed in its neat time-defying coffin. However, the most important consideration that suggested the Cooking Meta Toy to us is the fact that *relationship* often ameliorates or deteriorates around the table, when differences in taste become an issue. Taste is greatly influenced by cultural and personal habits. We can change our taste, but this change is limited by our basic individual make-up. For instance, among those people who cannot digest milk, some do, after drinking it for a while, develop the enzymes necessary to digest it. Others never do. A scientific experiment was conducted among normal subjects using sodium benzoate, an ingredient sometimes used as a preservative in catsup and other condiments. It was found that to some people it tastes bitter, to others sweet; others pronounced it salty, sour or tasteless!*

This experiment did not take into consideration the different responses to foods based on quantity, texture and temperature or the amazing influence smell and visual stimuli have on taste.

Let's imagine a family of five, each with different taste reactions, sitting at the dinner table. They take their first bites from a carefully prepared dish, and in unison say:

It's sweet!

It's bitter!

It's sour!

* *You Are Extraordinary*, Roger Williams. Random House, 1967.

It's salty!

It's tasteless!

No wonder each one thinks the other four bizarre, to say the least! How can people with such varied reactions, so deeply real to each, relate harmoniously? By accepting, rather than trying to change or tolerate, their diversity. Such acceptance may evolve into an understanding of differences in opinion, in feeling, in style of living. In the vast universe of our being, taste buds are as good a point as any other at which to improve relationships. We believe that the Cooking Meta Toy concept is singularly suited to ushering in this improvement. As you will see with Meta Toys One and Two, their combination, and Roulette, each of those five people could make his personal recipe, not just for one meal but for many.

Meta Toy One

Meta Toy One is composed of three rows of containers of different sizes placed on a lazy Susan.

On the inner circle the eight bottles contain:

> dried apricots
> prunes
> dates
> peaches
> figs
> raisins
> currants
> bran

On the larger circle, there are twelve containers filled with:

> pumpkin seeds
> sunflower seeds
> walnuts
> Spanish peanuts
> pignolas
> cashews
> filberts

steel-cut oats
pecans
macadamia nuts
almonds
Brazil nuts

The six small outer bottles contain seeds of:

chia
sesame
flax
caraway
flower pollen
psyllium

According to the way you combine these basic elements, you can make a crafty protein dish or a light fruit drink; you can make a complete meal—breakfast, lunch or dinner—or a sweet nourishing dessert. In addition to the ingredients contained in Meta Toy One, I always have some citrus fruits and juices on hand.

Obviously, freshly squeezed juices are best, but some of the frozen or concentrated juices which you find in health-food stores have no additives and are quite genuine and tasty. If it spurs your fancy to taste figs, cherries, strawberries and raspberries in winter, their concentrated juices maintain many of their original qualities.

It would take a computer to figure how many hundreds or thousands of recipes you can invent from the basic foods of Meta Toy One. Just to start you off, I will give you some of my favorites. It often happens, however, that I can't repeat a favorite recipe because I don't keep track of proportions. This may happen to you too; then you can easily create another favorite! I make most of my recipes with no more than five ingredients. When we put too many flavors together, they often cancel and distort rather than enhance one another.

These recipes are best made in a blender—Aldous called it a "whirligig." The ingredients can be coarsely or finely ground according to taste, in a matter of seconds. (If you don't have a blender or an electric nut grinder, a hand grinder will do.)

The recipes can be used for several purposes: as quickly ready snacks, as dessert and as breakfast. If you want a smooth dessert, blend the mixture until it has the texture of a mousse or a custard, put in champagne glasses and refrigerate until used. You may have to add a little liquid (water, juice or milk, raw certified please).

Dishes made with these ingredients are highly nutritional. The amount of protein is remarkable and rivals that of meat and eggs. The carbohydrates are of the highest quality; many of these foods are complete in themselves. If you are interested in these important food values, make your recipe according to your taste—then look up the chemical tables. You will be surprised and pleased to discover that your dish is not only tasty, but extremely nutritional. You can hardly go wrong with a Cooking Meta Toy made of the most refined gifts of earth, air, water and sun! What cook can produce an apricot, an almond or any of the seeds and fruits which nature—the most extravagantly imaginative cook of all—creates? The joyful and discreet mixing of these wonders can only produce another wonder. So go ahead. It is almost impossible to make a mistake. I know! I am not a cook and yet what I prepare with the Cooking Meta Toy delights my friends.

The greatest fun is when each member of the family creates his own recipe. The inventiveness of children is amazing when given this opportunity. Here are a few starters.

The dried fruits can either be presoaked in water, or water can be added while blending. To presoak dry fruit just cover it with boiling water and let it stand in a closed container. Use the juice when blending.

THE CHIA QUARTET

Blend:
> orange juice (fresh or frozen with no sugar added)
> prunes
> sunflower seeds
> chia seeds

THE PUMPKIN DUET

Blend dried figs and pumpkin seeds

THE FILBERT TRIO

Blend:
> sunflower seeds
> filberts
> cherry juice

THE RAISIN TRIO

Blend:
> dried peaches
> raisins
> pumpkin seeds

THE WALNUT QUARTET

Blend:
> dried figs
> currants
> orange juice
> walnuts

ALMOND DUET

Blend almonds and dried apricots

But the sweetest is the

DATE DUET

pecans and pitted dates

The pecans are cozily tucked inside the dates. If you prefer a drink: add enough liquid (water, milk or a fruit juice) and blend to the desired consistency.

Grated apple is a very good topping for all of these dishes. Also tiny pieces of lemon, orange or lime rind on top improve looks and fragrance.

Now make your own combination!

BREAKFAST ALL DAY

This is one of my favorites.

It is a crafty dish that will keep you at a high energy level for hours, preventing that irritation and exhaustion that makes you reach for coffee or cigarettes in the middle of the morning—besides it is good at any time of day.

Prepare it the night before you plan to eat it.

Place in a bowl one spoonful each of:

steel-cut oats
bran
sesame seed
flax seed
sunflower seed

Grind finely or coarsely, according to your taste, approximately:

10 almonds
5 filberts
a handful of pignolas
3 walnuts
3 pecans

Cut in small pieces five dried figs (or prunes) and five dried apricots (or peaches). Add a few raisins or currants.

Mix all ingredients with a wooden spoon or with your hands: the mixing is a treat to the eye! Cover with water and leave overnight at room temperature or, if you wish a softer texture, leave over pilot light. In the morning this complete meal will be a gentle welcome to your day. It will give your taste buds surprising delights of texture and taste.

If you prefer a liquid breakfast put the mixture in the "whirligig" and you will have an exotic, powerful drink. Sip it slowly while seeing with your mind's eye each nut and fruit and seed you are ingesting. Such a concentrated meal if drunk quickly may be difficult to digest and lose some of its value by not combining with the important enzymes in the mouth.

Experiment with your own different mixtures, and when you have decided on your favorite combination of seeds, nuts and dried fruits, prepare enough for a week or two and keep in a dry, tight jar in the refrigerator. Then take out only the needed quantity and cover with water for a while or overnight—if you like to chew long and well, use it immediately.

Meta Toy Two

This is a smaller Meta Toy, again on a lazy Susan.
Six bottles contain:

> olive oil
> apple-cider vinegar
> olive oil with shallots
>   garlic
>   onions
>   basil and garlic

Six smaller bottles contain:

> olive oil with chopped parsley
>   tiny pieces of lime
>   chopped chives
>   curry powder
> grated Parmesan
> capers

Fresh herbs (to be used whenever possible) keep fresh
for a considerable length of time when steeped in oil. It is
important to use an abundant quantity of these herbs.
Retrieving the herbs from Cooking Meta Toy Two is no

problem. I use stainless-steel iced-tea spoons, which can be left in the oil. They are long enough to stir and bring out the herbs that settle on the bottom. Use containers with large openings.

The purpose of Cooking Meta Toy Two is to make it possible for each member of the family to create his own recipe right at the table. Suppose your meal includes any of the following foods prepared without special condiment:

beans
rice
barley
pasta
hard-boiled eggs
salad (any kind)
steamed vegetables
steamed potatoes
tomatoes
cheeses (ricotta, cottage, hoop, farmer)

Does any member of your family like his rice in the Eastern style? Curry oil, chopped chives and ground almonds (from Cooking Meta Toy One) will do it.

Is another leaning toward Italian food? Garlic oil, parsley oil, Parmesan and some cracked walnuts (from Cooking Meta Toy One) can be added to pasta for superb spaghetti.

Do you wish to give a spicy taste to your cottage cheese? Just mix it with basic parsley oil and add a few capers. Do the same with steamed potatoes or hard-boiled eggs.

The combinations of these oils and herbs can be amazingly numerous and varied. My favorite mixture is basil and garlic oil. Remember to add lots of herbs to the oil. Of course, fresh herbs are preferred, but dried ones will do.*

Another favorite of mine is lime oil: after the chopped lime has been in the oil for one or two days, a most refined aroma will emerge. A teaspoon of this oil on a raw or lightly steamed grated turnip is, to me, a greater delicacy than caviar.

Does plain barley, the daily staple of Epicurus, seem a little flat to you? Just add a few cracked pecans and Parmesan—that earthy taste will take you right into the country at sunrise.

If you wish to prepare a snack quickly for cocktails: Make a paste with Parmesan, basil and garlic oil (lots of basil) . Spread on thin-sliced bread or toast.

But enough of *my* recipes!

We devised the Meta Toys so you can have fun with your own personal recipes!

---

* My friends use these combinations of oils and herbs on fish and meat, boiled or broiled.

Meta Toys One and Two

The most interesting combinations are made with the items of Cooking Meta Toys One and Two, with which, my computer says, 3673 recipes are possible. Their distinctive features are that they are simple, potently nutritious and given personal flavor by the herbs.

These recipes are based on three elements:

oil
herbs
seeds and nuts

Freshly pressed vegetable oil and seed oil are the best source of fat, without which our body cannot function. Many oils, like safflower, sunflower seed, soybean and corn, contain essential unsaturated fatty acids, which are cholesterol-lowering agents. Olive oil is neutral in relation to cholesterol in that it neither augments nor diminishes it. I am partial to olive oil, but I suggest you experiment with others (cold-pressed and kept in a cool place) to widen the variety of your recipes.

Herbs, as well as giving character to food, have nutritional and healing qualities. Ancient medicine was based mainly on herbs. Because of their use as flavoring agents, we include in this category garlic, onion, shallot, ginger and horseradish.

Nuts have high nutritional value, but seeds have the highest—no wonder, since a little seed contains the elements which create a tree! In *The Complete Book of Food and Nutrition* J. I. Rodale writes:

> The seed is the crucible wherein the alchemy of life works its magic. In this tiny place is contained the condensed germinating energy, the life-giving elements, including as yet undiscovered gleams. Science still knows very little of the vast and intricate interplay of life forces that lie within the seed. . . .
>
> Thomas H. Mather, writing in *Scientific Agriculture,* Vol. 10, 1929, about an experiment in which the effect of a chemical fertilizer, superphosphate, was measured on a crop of alfalfa, in comparison with a similar crop on which no fertilizer was used, discovered that all of the inorganic phosphorus of the fertilizer went to the stalk and leaves. In this experiment it was proven that the seed actually turned back the inorganic phosphorus. It would have none of it. Nature cannot build a strong race of alfalfa plants with minerals that are inorganic. If there is not sufficient supply of organic minerals, the plant will either produce seed which is defective, or it will not produce seed at all.*

From the above it seems that seeds have a keener sense of nutritional values than we have! What mysterious faculty makes the unborn seed refuse life unless it meets a certain standard?

* *The Complete Book of Food and Nutrition,* J. I. Rodale and staff. Rodale Books, Inc., 1961.

In any case, edible seeds have unsurpassed nutritional value. As in high-protein diets based on animal food, the following recipes have a high content of protein which burns the fats to generate energy. Recipes composed of seeds, nuts, oil and herbs are blended in the "whirligig" and their thickness is regulated by the addition of liquid: with oil alone they produce rich sauces; with the addition of a little milk, yogurt or vegetable stock they can be served as soup. If you prefer them as thin dressings you can add a little water without diminishing the concentrated taste. I don't mention salt in the following recipes, but it can be added at any time to suit your taste. Also keep lemon and lime juice and apple cider vinegar handy to provide an accent on individual taste. If you wish to experiment with small quantities, put herbs and nuts or seeds in a coffee or nut grinder; make a paste and add liquids.

Here are some examples of high-protein herb and nut recipes.

Blend one of the following combinations until smooth:

> lemon and lime juice
> macadamia nuts
> parsley (a lot)
> parsley in garlic oil

> walnuts
> garlic oil
> oregano
> apple cider vinegar (a few drops)

> almonds
> curry oil
> lemon juice

lime oil and one small piece of lime
sunflower seeds
capers (add after blending)

oil
cashews
chives and/or parsley
cider vinegar

basil oil
pecans
grated Parmesan
lime juice
parsley

Roulette

One reason for putting the Meta Toys on a lazy Susan is that it is a practical way to enable everyone to reach each container. Another reason is adventure-inspired: one can make new recipes by playing "Roulette."

As you see, the little statue between the two roulettes is a dancing lady—she is Chinese and ageless. A creature of charm and wisdom, she is curtsying to her favorite lover and pointing to the food she has prepared for him. She has, and *is,* the expression of unerring taste and that is why I sometimes let her choose the ingredients for a new recipe: I whirl both toys and when they stop I choose the ingredients nearest to her. One of the combinations chosen by the Chinese lady is, amazingly enough, a well-known Italian recipe called *pesto:*

> basil (a lot) and garlic oil
> pignolas
> grated Parmesan
> a dash of cider vinegar

Blend in the "whirligig" until very smooth. Serve on

pasta or rice, or with vegetables. I have yet to meet someone who is not enthusiastic about this recipe!

If you don't have a dancing Chinese lady to play
"Roulette," a flower or your favorite object can serve as
pointer. Spin your roulettes: you can only win!

Making a Cooking Meta Toy

My Cooking Meta Toys are just two models which I made to fit my taste and style. Have fun building yours to fit *your* taste and style. You may want to have several Meta Toys—or consolidate all ingredients into one large setup. I have seen smooth, wide lazy Susans in Chinese family restaurants. Or you may fancy a vertical Meta Toy in several tiers, a spicy, whirling tower.

From the empty containers you will soon know what your family and friends prefer. Almost anyone is happy to be given a sudden and easy chance to experiment and invent, especially when the results are invariably excellent. Children and young brides who never cooked before make sensational combinations at their first trial. A family or group of friends can invent new recipes together, not according to words, weights and measures, but according to the immediate experience of taste. We realize that our differences in taste need not be an obstacle to good relationships, but can actually be a stimulating influence. Your Cooking Meta Toy will be a mandala: a center for fun and communication—*a Mangia Mandala!*

Note: To make my Cooking Meta Toy I shopped in

those popular import shops which have wide and varied stock of glass containers from all over the world.

Part Three

Sometimes we think that other people are self-assured and doubt-free while we are vulnerable and unsafe, and feel a disconcerting quivering within Our Trembling Ego.

We often forget that probably every person, at times and under certain circumstances, feels His Trembling Ego. In fact, often those who seem most self-assured *might be the victims, not just of ego tremors, but of veritable earthquakes which they have had to learn to hide from the world's curious eyes.*

How many human beings?

How many Trembling Egos?

ALL LIVING IS RELATIONSHIP

Invitation

In *Island,* a manual on the Art of Living and Loving and Dying, Aldous stressed relationship at every opportunity.

> Never give children a chance of imagining that anything exists in isolation. Make it plain that all living is relationship. Show them relationships in the woods, in the fields, in the ponds and streams, in the village and the country around it.

In the last few years, ecology has become a household word. It simply means the study of the relationships between any organism and its environment—what exists but organisms and their environment? A molecule is an organism, a galaxy is an organism, so are flies and humming-birds, carrots and snakes, tulips and eagles, dolphins, protozoa and ourselves.

This is an invitation to the following series of recipes designed to deepen our awareness of the oneness of living, relating and changing.

Since all relationship will be benefited by an improved relationship with ourselves and with infinity, it is best to experience the first two recipes for a month—"Be Your Own Ideal Parents" and "Mystery Suspended among Infinities." Many of our problems with others depend on how we feel about ourselves. And we all relate better with the situation here-now if we are aware of the infinity of time and space before and after us.

While you experience these two recipes, read the others several times: your choice of a recipe for *Relationship with Others* will probably change as you experience "Be Your Own Ideal Parents" and "Mystery Suspended among Infinities."

There is no specification or limitation as to whether the persons involved are related by blood, marriage or circumstances.

RELATIONSHIP WITH ONESELF

Be Your Own Ideal Parents

Ideal parents are such a rarity that we can practically say they are nonexistent. But a real possibility exists for each of us to be our own ideal parent. This is one of the most effective ways to improve our relationship with ourselves.

We often hear of the distress of parents who, having devoted all they had to the upbringing of their children, feel sadly disappointed by the results. Their vision of what that child could or should have become is shattered by reality. Just as often, the same disappointment occurs in children and adolescents. They too had an image of their ideal parents, an image that was shattered again and again. Mutual disappointment in each other often troubles the relationship between parents and children and consequently the relationship of each person to himself.

At any age the discovery that we can become our own ideal parents is momentous and improves all relationship.

First we must let go of dependence on our parents, whether they are present or absent, loved or unloved, living or dead. We may be unaware of this emotional dependence which can be deeply buried or on the surface, expressing itself either in rebellion against or in blind conformity to the parents' wishes, opinions and emotions.

Each of us has probably imagined the ideal father or the ideal mother he would like (or would have liked) to have. This father is a paragon of excellence. His qualities include a tremendous interest in and comprehension of ME. How proud *I* am of him! And how delighted with and full of praise for *me* he is! We imagine overhearing our father telling a friend what a wonderful human being his son or daughter is. When the ideal father is severe and even punishing, how justly so! We are even grateful for that just punishment because it is given in a way that relieves our guilt, rather than diminishing or discouraging our self-confidence. His fair punishment makes us feel more secure and ready to go ahead, having learned something very important which might otherwise have taken years and years to learn. This father, although a busy and important man, always has time if we need him, to answer questions, to discuss a viewpoint, to lend a hand in a project.

And our ideal mother? She glows with happy love for the only man who could have given her that very special child—ME! There is a constant unspoken alliance of mother and child to give the father more love, just as there is a constant unspoken alliance of father and child to cherish and protect this unbelievably lovable woman. It is not necessary to tell her our fears, desires, uncertainties or dreams. She knows—and assuages, reassures and restores our confidence in ourselves and in life. We almost cry when we think of her tenderness. Yes, we cry, overwhelmed by emotion at the thought of our ideal parents. It is marvelous to have such a mother and father, and we are completely aware of our good luck.

It is a rare occurrence to have ideal parents. If you did, you don't need this recipe. I assume you belong to the great majority whose parents did the best they could, yet were not the ideal, the perfect parents. Even if they were endowed with the highest qualities, it would be almost impossible for a child to realize it: not having experienced the *absence* of something makes it difficult to recognize its *presence*. Whichever the case, looking for ideals is a high human privilege.

The fact that we look for ideal parents is not in any way to be interpreted as a criticism of our real parents. They did the best they could, having been brought up by their parents, under circumstances mostly unknown to us. Have we thought or tried to imagine how our parents were as newborn babies, as children, as adolescents? How *their* parents were acting and feeling? That time-space seems to us more distant than the moon—after all, we have seen the moon and we have seen *living* human beings walking on it. The records of our parents' infancy and childhood are scant in comparison, generally nonexistent. To criticize our parents, of whom we have such incomplete knowledge, such a one-sided view, would be unjust and unintelligent.

To interpret this recipe as a criticism of parents or parent substitutes would distort it completely. If you feel that you may do so, experience the "YES–NO–YES" recipe first and then come back to this one. In any case, realize that the point of this recipe is *not to compare, but to create*.

Directions:

> Consider a situation in your present life that is difficult or perplexing, or any situation you might wish to improve.
>
> Do not choose a situation involving your parents.

If my description fits your ideal parents, read it again, enlarge on it and go into it deeply.

If my description does not correspond to your ideal, build your own image of them:
>Imagine your Ideal Mother.
>See your Ideal Mother.
>Hear your Ideal Mother.
>Smell your Ideal Mother.
>Touch your Ideal Mother.

Take time in contacting each sensation.

Create your Ideal Mother in every detail.

Now consider the situation which you have chosen before, and listen for your Ideal Mother's reaction and suggestions. Listen to her words.

Speak them aloud with her tone of voice.

Your contact with her is so close, you feel her so keenly, that the expression of her face, her voice, her body melts into yours.

Express in a bodily position this conscious merging of the essential quality of your Ideal Mother with yours.

Assume a bodily position which expresses the attitude of your Ideal Mother toward you. Assume this position in every detail: fingers, mouth, eyebrows, etc.

Remain in this position for five minutes or longer.

Follow the same directions with your Ideal Father.

Your Ideal Parents give you advice and courage and a deeper sense of yourself and of your unique identity. You feel this in the depth of your bodymind. Above all, you feel their unconditional love for you.

No matter what you do, what you are, whether you follow their advice or not, they love you, they sustain you, they are *for* you. Above all, they implore you to love and respect yourself. If you are not yet able to do so completely, they keep on loving you until you indeed love and respect yourself as much as they do. You see, hear, feel those two ideal human beings that have created you. Your communion with them is so close that you become aware of their existence within you—for they are *you.*

And now that you are your own ideal parents, you have a clearer and deeper understanding of your own children, for you are also *Your Own Child.*

*Many persons read and collect recipes for preparing food,
but until a recipe is carried out, its ingredients mixed and
cooked, it cannot be experienced. The recipe itself cannot
be eaten. It is in its application that the edible result is
produced. The same principle applies to these recipes for
living and loving. Reading will acquaint you with them
intellectually, but it is only by putting them into practice
that you can experience them. There are several ways to
put these recipes into practice:*

One way is to have and to be a supporting partner.

*Another—the most practical way—is to make your own
recording of the recipes. This was suggested in the prologue and is repeated here because it is such an effective
method. It is gratifying to have your personal tape library
always available. I remember how Aldous enjoyed listening to poetry which he had read aloud into a tape recorder.*

*Another effective procedure is to carry out the recipes
within a small, attuned group. One person reads aloud and
the group follows the instructions. The reader must be
sensitive in his timing because there can be considerable
differences in the personal rhythm of the members of even
a small group.*

Mystery Suspended among Infinities

Psychology has given little or no consideration to infinity, and to our relationship with it. And yet we are immersed in it. Our field of action on this planet might be only a few miles, but all around this field is the infinite and the unknown. Our life lasts a few dozen years, but time before and time after is unlimited, as far as we know and can imagine. Suspended among infinities, we spend our lives, absorbed in our everyday business, and we tend to ignore what is or might be all around our limited energy field. If a fuller integration is to be achieved, our sense of infinity and our relationship with it has to be cultivated.

If we deeply consider the fact of infinity around and within ourselves, we are bound to be awed almost to the degree of paralysis. We might come to the nihilistic point where, as Marcus Aurelius said, "Nothing is of any import. Seen in the light of infinity, all things become equally insignificant." Yet we think that this approach is a finite view of infinity. The attitude that "it is all the same" may, for some, be a tempting risk, but certainly is not the final word. The more we learn to feel infinity within and without, the more a sense of liberation and lightness pervades us. When our relationship with infinity deepens, it dissolves our finite concepts of comparative measures of space and time.

Directions:

Keep your eyes closed throughout. Without turning, see with your mind's eye what is to your right, very close to you: objects, a table, the wall. Imagine each object in detail. Feel it, as if you were touching it.

And now expand further.

Keep imagining what is in your right hemisphere, but in a slightly wider range. What is there beyond the wall?

What is there beyond your house?

the street?

the surrounding area?

Be in the street.

Be in the surrounding area.

See people walking, feel the flavor of their life.

Look how they move: are they running toward a goal?

Do they know what they are doing?

Look at them: observe them, as well as the feelings they evoke in you.

Now leave that street. Go further out of the city into the country.

Feel the difference in the air, in the physical and psychological pressure around you.

Keep expanding now, always on the right side.

Now you are expanding further, you go through an ocean, through the immense marine life and its undulating vegetation.

You encounter strange unknown creatures.

Go through.

Keep going.

Go to another country where people speak a language unknown to you.

Look at these people.

Observe their feelings and your reaction to them.

Now you go through a vast desert, always to your right, and through snowcapped mountains.

Keep expanding until you go off the earth and find the sky.

Go through the peaceful, clear sky.

Through menacing clouds and luminous clouds.

Through the dazzling light of the sun.

Through into galactic space, and further into other galaxies, into ever-expanding infinity.

Then, quite fast, come back right here, where you are. Compare now the different feeling on your left and on your right side.

Then proceed in the same way for the left side.

Now it is time to expand downwards. Consider what lies under you: first, the chair on which you are sitting. Feel its tactile sensation, your weight on it, and then expand further down: to the floor, under it, to the earth.

Take time to feel what the underground is like: some of it damp and cold; some of it rocky, hard; some of it teeming with life.

As you go deeper, you contact fragments of past civilizations, fossils, buried and forgotten remnants from the past.

Go deeper, toward the center of the earth, coming near to fire—red, stirring incandescence.

You are now reaching the very core of the earth, forever exploding.

Now from the center of the earth you are advancing toward its surface on the other side, at your antipodes.

Again, you find ancient strata, a variety of levels of silent and dark consistency, and then again the light of day.

What is at your antipodes? A big busy town? A deeply blue ocean? A desert? The country? A stadium? The living room of an ancient house where two old ladies are gossiping?

Keep reaching down: now you will find again the sky, the clouds, and then infinite space. Once more, with your sensory terminals, reach the galaxies.

Now you are back in your room, sitting in your armchair.

Expand now upwards, in the same way as you have expanded in all other directions.

Now consider infinity in time—go back in your imagination to what happened yesterday. See some of that in detail. Then jump back to a distant event in your childhood. Visualize how everybody you know looks.

Everybody around you is younger. You are a little child. People are there who actually have been dead for quite a while. Go back in time, to when they were children.

Look at the people in the streets: they are dressed differently, talk differently, move differently.

Go back in time: choose some ancient civilization now.

Go still further back, to the prehistoric eras of cavemen. Further back through the evolutionary process in any way you know it or feel it—through man's ancestry, through the immense primitive forms of life; and then further to the single-cell organism.

Imagine a time still earlier when there is no animate life, not even vegetation. The earth is primal ocean of undifferentiated matter.

Follow the earth to its very beginning, go before its birth to whatever astral shape from which it was born—a foaming, whirling cloud of gases.

Go back in time to the beginningless beginning: a beginning that recedes back into ever-expanding infinity.

Come back to the here-now; in your armchair, in your room.

Begin to project into the future. Consider yourself tomorrow and in the following days.

What are your projects?

See yourself in a few years, say ten. Things have changed; you are older, you have lived longer and have accumulated greater experience.

What are you doing?

Where are you living?

Look around you at your dear ones: they have changed too.

Some of them are no longer there.

Now see yourself as a very old person.

Look into your eyes.

Go into the time when you no longer exist in your present form. It is the world of the future, the world that is going on independently of you.

Some part of you has survived: Maybe your portrait on somebody's desk? Maybe your words, your children, your deeds?

Maybe a sense of presence, in the room where you used to live?

Maybe a recollection of you in the words or smiles of the ones who have survived you?

But even that passes. Imagine now our civilization in a very distant future. There is no longer even a trace of you, of your home, of your dear ones and friends, of anything you know that exists now. Imagine a future civilization, a million years hence, totally different from our present one.

Now let this planet come to an end. A planetary catastrophe is taking place; you can see planet Earth exploding in space.

You are transported to another planet with different forms of life than the one to which you may belong.

Now you leave that too; you are in space among stars and galaxies. Extend your mind to the most distant future that you can conceive, and know that after that, there is still infinite time to come.

Return to the present time, and see yourself suspended among infinities.

Now imagine a small bright point of light in front of your eyes, a few inches away from you.

Let this point extend until it engulfs your head, and then your whole body. Your whole body is now inside this ethereal sphere. The expansion is now going in all directions of time and space and it is going faster and faster. It includes the whole room, and then all of the surroundings. This sphere is expanding in space and time. The center is widening in all directions. Experience this widening as being continuous, all-inclusive, gently pervasive. Again, extend to the far-off boundaries of the universe, and then to infinity. Let everything be included in the sphere now: all timeless space, everything that ever was and ever will be.

Then, at a simple snap of your fingers, the infinite sphere will contract instantaneously into a very little luminous point in front of you, carrying infinity within.

Look at that point in front of you. It is the Aleph; it contains all the points of the universe, and the universe seen from all possible points. It is the All. Take that little point of light, and put it a few inches above your head, and let it dwell there, over you—you, mystery suspended among infinities.

In a good relationship, criticism is a sign of affectionate interest not interpreted as a "cutting down" but as a "building up." The contrary is true in a disturbed relationship.

RELATIONSHIP WITH OTHERS

A Moving Sea

. . . make not a bond of love:
Let it rather be a moving sea between
the shores of your souls.
—Kahlil Gibran
  The Prophet

With the poet's genius for synthesis, Gibran describes in these few words the ideal relationship between two people, and emphasizes the feeling of the environment in which this relationship exists.

Science has come to the conclusion (field theory) that nothing exists separated from the environment. While our sense of being individuals is real and indisputable, so is the fact that, as individuals, we exist in relation to the air we breathe, the food we eat, the sounds of waves by which we hear, and other beings with whom we create and partake of the environment. As Alan Watts clearly puts it: "The human being inside the skin and the world outside the skin are regarded as having in the skin a common boundary which belongs to both."

In the following recipes we will limit ourselves to the relationship between two people. However, let us remain aware that no relationship exists in a vacuum: each is incessantly influenced by the environment from which it receives much of its flair and character. Two persons living in the ghetto of a megalopolis would interact differently were they living on the open sea. And a person's view of himself and of his environment influences the quality of his interaction with others.

Choose a relationship you wish to improve. Let's go back to Gibran's image of *a moving sea between the shores*. For the time being we will not consider the quality of the shores, but only of the water in between.

> *Reflect on the quality of the relationship rather than on yourself and the other person. This relationship is represented by the moving sea. Visualize its color, quality, quantity; feel its temperature, its movement. Read the list below, and when one characteristic elicits a reaction, close your eyes and go into it.*

> Is the moving sea between the shores of your souls:
> stagnant water?
> abundant water?
> tempestuous water?
> scarce water?
> torpid water?
> limpid water?
> cold water?
> fragrant water?
> stimulating?
> icy?
> boiling?
> polluted?
> intensely blue?
> grayish?

> Does the moving sea contain:
> small ice blocks?

immense icebergs?
fishes?
vegetation?
boulders?
human beings?
corpses?
a monster?
a nymph or a siren?
a sunken ship? If so, explore it.

Is the moving sea:
a pond? Are there any petals floating on its surface?
the primal sea from which we all came ages ago?
the fluid in which we had our being before entering the world of air?
holy water?

Make your own addition to this list.

After you have become more aware of the *flavor* of the relationship, you will know how much it depends on you and the other person, and how much it is influenced by others and by the environment.

The Cruelty of Unawareness: "How Can I See What Is Right in Front of Me?"

A good hypnotic subject can be given a post-hypnotic suggestion that for the next two hours he will behave in a totally normal manner, except for one thing: he will be completely unaware of the presence of any person dressed in red. The subject will do exactly that. Should the person in a fire-red suit speak, he will not hear. The person could be standing in front of him and the subject will not see him. That person could even touch our subject and he will not feel him.

To what extent are the dilemmas, sadness and tragedies of human relations due to unawareness? We speak with horror of the large-scale cruelty of murder, illness and poverty. The cruelty due to unawareness, although of a subtler nature, is just as destructive, poignant and omnipresent.

We rarely hurt, or are hurt, with fully conscious malice. Most wounds are inflicted by negligence, inattention, egocentrism—in short, by the cruelty of unawareness.

However, the cruelty of unawareness insidiously coexists with valuable qualities and a desire to influence people in a way which we imagine is good for them, without our understanding of the differences between human beings. If this unawareness is extreme it becomes cruel, in spite of pure intention and loving feeling. For instance, just imagine a strong, muscular young man, with a natural need for movement and wide spaces, being induced into a white-collar career, imprisoned at a desk eight hours a day! No wonder a tremendous tension builds up in such a person's bodymind! This tension will explode either inside, in some form of illness (digestive or heart trouble, a displaced disk, addiction to alcohol or other drugs, depression, etc.), or outside, in some form of violence or apathy. Unawareness initiated the illness and/or the violence.

At times we are unaware of subtle feelings, but often we are just as unaware of what is obvious to everyone else— blatant and loud, as a person dressed in blazing red.

We might not be aware of the fact that some dear one is missing us, because we are giving all our energy and attention to our favorite occupation. We might overlook the fact that somebody is being hurt by our words just because all of our attention is devoted to what we are saying and not to the effect that our words might have on the other person. We might frighten someone with no intention of doing so.

"Our business is to wake up," Aldous wrote a few days before dying.* In six words he expressed a whole life program.

This recipe on unawareness in relationship is part of that program.

* *This Timeless Moment,* Laura Huxley. Farrar, Straus & Giroux, 1968.

Directions:

> Consider a relationship which you feel could be satisfactory, yet leaves much to be desired. "Take the bull by the horns," as the saying goes. Simply ask the relating person, "What do I overlook in our relationship which is obvious to you?" Listen attentively to the answer: even if you don't agree with it, don't react immediately. Take time to think about it.
>
> Keep thinking of this person while completing orally or in writing the following statements. Do this as fast as you can, without reflecting on what you are saying: let the very first spontaneous answer emerge.
>
> It suddenly occurred to me that . . .
> I finally discovered that . . .
> I was shocked to find out that . . .
> For years I have not been aware of . . .
> I am constantly avoiding . . .
> I'd rather not . . .
> Even if nobody agrees, I will finally . . .
>
> Then direct your subconscious to work on your problem. Before going to sleep give your intense attention for five minutes to this subject: "In which way today have I been aware in my relationship with _____?"
>
> Don't let this concentrated thinking turn into a daydream or a chest-beating Mea Culpa! That would defeat the purpose of this recipe. If there is any danger of wallowing in guilt, you'd better experience "YES–NO–YES" first. (An example of the other general danger in thinking about unawareness is to lament the fate of five million children starving thousands of miles away, instead of being aware that the baby here and now needs a new diaper.)
>
> Your intense, evening concentration will probably elicit significant dreams. Notice above all the feelings in the dreams and listen to their message.
>
> Alternate the practice of this recipe with "Be a Birth Giver."

Only by listening to criticism with objectivity and attention can we decide whether to accept it and use it.

Our Instant Reactions

Relationships are damaged or improved by:

words and voice inflection

threshold level of resistance to sounds, silence, music

appearances

smells

differences in temperament (see "Facts and Feelings")

differences in taste (music, literature, art, food, etc.)

intensity of reactions

image of what the relationship should be

Our senses react instantaneously to words, appearances, sounds, smells, vibrations. Frequently this reaction prevents our perceiving deeper human qualities, or colors our reception of them. We live through our senses. A smell can give us heavenly pleasure or, conversely, it can awaken fear and repulsion. Although the way we speak, look, sound, smell and dress is not our very essence, it is an extension of our being. Sometimes we react to others through this extension only—and dismiss the essence of the person.

It does not seem *right* to let our liking or loving be influenced by sensations only, yet they do influence us to a great extent. Sensations are a vital part of all relationships —good or bad, deep or superficial—and it is valuable to find, in an unsatisfactory relationship, whether a sensation is the upsetting cause.

Visual impressions are usually the first and strongest. In this context it is fascinating to see how fashion shapes many facets of our life and relationship. Fashion persuaded woman, at different epochs, to flatten her chest or, conversely, to encourage its super-pendulousness; to cinch her waist with strangulating corsets; to displace her inner organs by wearing high-heeled shoes. All these and other eccentricities were intended to make her body more attractive. So the fashion was followed, causing physiological harm comparable to that caused by those heavy metal rings that pierce the noses of primitive African tribesmen.

Beautiful and idealistic young people often masquerade as derelicts in order to follow, not their aesthetic sense, but the command of fashion imposed by their peers, and dictated by a feeling of pseudo-independence.

Older people, especially men, have put themselves in funereal suits to show that they belong to the respectable, intellectual class.

As long as we know that we are playing a game, these masquerades are not damaging—they may even be amusing —but what a disaster for our relationships if we take the game seriously! Just imagine a father discussing a personal problem or opinion with a teen-age son, each dressed according to the most extreme fashion of his peers, each in a garb more antagonistically disparate than were the uniforms of a Prussian soldier and one of Napoleon's hussars facing each other on the battlefield. If the two soldiers lost their uniforms and came upon one another naked, their visually dictated impulse to kill each other would probably vanish. How helpful it would be for parents and children to discuss important personal problems naked, or if more comfortable, dressed in simple and similar tunics! Why not take an empty grain sack, make holes for the head and the arms, and discuss difficult and really turbulent problems of relationship dressed alike? Compassion, understanding and humor would be awakened through this absence of exterior differences.

We certainly do not advocate uniformity of dress. On the contrary, it is good and interesting for each person to dress in the way he feels more at ease. We only mean that, in times of dissent, it is desirable to go to the root of the matter and eliminate exterior and distracting trappings.

Sometimes it is difficult to discover why a relationship is becoming inharmonious or losing vitality. These questions will help:

> *On which point does this relationship disintegrate?*
>
> *When is it at its best?*
>
> *Read the following list quickly, and mark the item which leaps to your consciousness as the stimulant of dissent—*
>> *words?*
>> *sex?*
>> *smell?*
>> *clothes?*
>> *looks?*
>> *friends?*
>> *voice quality?*
>> *voice inflection?*
>> *silence?*
>> *taste?*
>> *demonstration of affection?*
>> *vibrations?*

One of these may emerge at first sight as the cause of the disturbed relationship. It may be just the most easily perceived tip of a deep iceberg. This is not always so, but it is at times. In a deeply disturbed relationship, everything and nothing may be a stimulant and give cause to an outburst of blind passion. This outburst can be the initial step toward clarification and resolution. Whether this happens or not, practice the recipe "Be a Birth Giver."

If all suggestions, comments or criticisms make you feel that you are the target of accusations, it is urgent to find what, in your inner world, motivates such a wearisome and persistent reaction.

Play with Dynamite

A relationship may disintegrate because of a personal difference in understanding words, or a different level of skill in expressing feelings in words. How often we have felt crushed by not being understood simply because we were unable to make the other person feel what we really meant, unable to find words that communicated our intense and subtle feelings. Or, if our words seemed expressive to us, they did not *speak* to the other person.

These forms that we set down on paper to make words—those that we construct with lips and tongue and through which, by adding a flow of air, spoken words come into existence—how powerful they are! Much of our lives depends on them.

Just as words are a step in our evolution from the more general and primitive sounds used by animals, so nonverbal communication may be the next evolutionary process. Nonverbal communication, like telepathy, is beginning to be accepted and explored, even by those scientific disciplines which not long ago refused to admit its existence.

The awareness of what words directed at us do *to us* will open our awareness of the impact that our own words have on other persons. Words often have a different meaning for the person who hears them than for the person who says them. They may create disturbing echoes of one's own past; they have the power of an unrecognized enemy. But words are not the only offenders: inflection and tone of voice can change their meaning.

Take, for instance, the word "really." It can be said with an inflection that will give the impression that you are consumed with admiration for the perspicacity and knowledge of the person with whom you are speaking. Or it can be said with a tone meaning "I don't believe a word you say." Which may be interpreted as "You are a liar." Or it can express unbearable boredom. Think of all the different qualities you can put into saying "yes" and "no." Two capital words that can change your life! Often we say "yes" in a way that means "no"—and vice versa.

Throughout this recipe we will speak of *the word,* meaning the word or phrase which gives us a toxic reaction. Such a word or phrase is like dynamite—let's use it with awareness instead of being blown up when we least expect it. Here are several recipes to deal with *the word.*

DYNAMITE ONE:

Decide which is the word.

Take a roll of shelf paper and a felt-tip pen. Write the word in every possible way that you can imagine: small, big, in your own writing or someone else's, printed in several assorted styles, calligraphy, in all colors and color combinations. Write each vowel and consonant separately. Now mix vowels and consonants and make new words with them, meaningful or meaningless. Spell the word backwards. Write it vertically or obliquely, upside

down—start from the top, the bottom, any side of the
sheet—write the word capriciously!

DYNAMITE TWO:

Become aware of the vowels and consonants of the word
as shapes—various interesting shapes that are really like
drawings. Draw the vowels and consonants of the word
not only with the pen but with your feeling as well. Keep
drawing consonants and vowels on your long, long shelf
paper—they might change into faces, places . . . a story
in pictures may come out of those vowels and consonants.

DYNAMITE THREE:

Say the word very slowly and voicelessly. Say it slower
and slower until you become aware of the amazing skill
required by your lips and tongue to form the word. Slower
and voicelessly, you discover the wonder of the human
capacity to make thousands of different meaningful
sounds with the infinite skill of tongue and lips. Now
you are saying the word so slowly that you feel the form
of each consonant and vowel. As an instance, let's take
the word "voicelessly" and form each sound separately
and voicelessly:

v
o
i
c
e
l
e
s
s
l
y

> Do this several times with the consonants and vowels of
> the word.

Aren't you amazed at the capacity you have to say thousands of words by making thousands of forms without even thinking about it? And there are thousands of different languages which require thousands of different forms from the human tongue and lips! How long, according to our chronological time, has it taken evolution to bring about this wonder of which we are hardly aware?

DYNAMITE FOUR:

> And now you are going to give voice to the word. You
> are beginning to know it from inside out. You speak it
> now in every different kind of tone.
>
> The inflection we give to words is sometimes more powerful than the word itself because it is more elusive.
>
> Take your word and say it with all possible inflections
> and tones, giving to it all possible significance, using your
> speaking voice as an instrument of selective expression.
> Say it in all the ways it has been said to you and in all the
> ways you would like to say it back, whispering or screaming.

DYNAMITE FIVE:

> Now you are going to energize the word with music.
> Either alone or accompanied by the music of your choice,
> you are going to sing the word; sing it in your own unique
> way, as though you were a baby hardly able to say it, just
> learning to say it—possibly with a babyish mispronunciation, or with the fire of youth, or the thoughtfulness of
> maturity. Again your inner world of memory, feelings and
> fantasy (not your voice or musical training) determines
> the limit of the ways you sing the word.

DYNAMITE SIX:

And now it is time to give your entire body to the word. You know it intellectually, emotionally, visually and vocally. Now with your entire body, you express that word or phrase in the most complete way: you dance it with your favorite music, taking any posture that expresses that word for you. As you dance, a posture will repeatedly emerge which unmistakably represents the feeling evoked by the word: hold that posture as long as you can—in fact, a little longer. Remain frozen in that position until your body begins to tremble. Let it tremble and shake. This is one of the most effective ways to let go of old tensions. Be happy if this shaking happens, for it is a deep release. But whether or not it happens, dance the word, and when you finally sing it while you dance it, you no longer will be affected by it. Dancing and singing the word, you realize your freedom from it.

Facts and Feelings

Beautiful relationships are often marred by ignoring fundamental differences between human beings. It is this very difference that often attracts people to each other and is the basis of deep relations. But unless this disparity is brought out in the light of consciousness and fully respected, the two persons will experience difficult times.

This situation often arises between two persons of opposite types, the *feeling* type and the *intellectual* type. One person is oriented on the emotional level, the other on the intellectual level.

The frustration of two people locked in such anguished dialogue is similar to a nightmare in which one shouts with all one's power, the chest almost bursting, without uttering a sound. There is never a person who is exclusively on the *feeling* level, or one who is exclusively on the *intellectual* level, but one trait can overrule the other. For the person who is dealing mostly with facts, everything is "out there." For the person dealing with feeling, everything is inside, unseen, and often inexpressible. The *feeling* person is usually less articulate than the *factual* intellectual. The frustration of not being able to express the intensity and subtlety of what he feels creates a vicious circle: the more he feels, the less he can express—therefore he keeps feeling more and more while expressing less and less, until he bursts. It may be a shout, or an abusive word, a destructive gesture or action, aggravating the situation by leaving it unfinished at the worst stage. In the meantime, the *fact* person, hurt and bewildered, despairs about communicating with a person who is so violent. It is difficult for the *fact* person to understand that, while facts are certainly important, they are only a fragment of reality. Facts should be considered in relation to the persons involved and to the time and place in which they occur. The *fact* person may well say, "But the fact remains that my husband threw on the floor his favorite lasagna over which I had worked all day." The "fact" is there, all over the floor. But how had this woman, unwittingly no doubt, frustrated and provoked the man into throwing on the floor the very food he was looking forward to eating?

I once witnessed an episode typical of two people speaking on two different levels: a mother and her fifteen-year-old son.

On a hot summer day, the mother enters her son's room. The room is in that unique kind of chaos that only teenagers can achieve. Adding to the confusion, a rock record is blasting away. The mother is hopelessly wandering about the room trying to pick up and put things in order. She finds an unfamiliar pair of pants, and, holding them up, she says, "Where did you get these horrible pants?!" They have gone through many battles, are patched, torn, unmended and dirty. They still show a trace of the voluptuous form of whoever had worn them. The son says, "They're not mine, they're Donna's, and they are not horrible—they're really nice pants." The mother, on edge with the confusion and the blasting noise, retorts, *"What is nice about them?* They are ugly, dirty, worn-out and spotted. How can you say they are nice?" The son, who is enjoying his recollection of the voluptuous girl who had been inside the pants, unconsciously feels that his mother is casting these epithets on the girl. This interpretation makes him belligerent and insistent on his point: "That doesn't make any difference, they are really nice pants."

Mother, definitely feeling that she now has indisputable proof of his irrationality, considers it to be her duty to bring forth his capacity to reason. "You see—" she says patiently, "pants are just like people. They can have their faults and it's fine to like them just the same. You may like them even when they are not nice." Innocently, she is giving him more and more reason to misinterpret her and to think that she is insulting his girl. Trying harder and harder to make him reason, she persists: "Just point out what's nice about these pants." Son and mother, getting louder and by now speaking at the same time, are no longer listening to one another. Defiantly, the son shouts: "O.K. I say they are nice pants!"

At this point the mother's factual approach to the pants abruptly gives way to a sudden view of the real situation, and she too is taken over by feelings of concerned responsibility. "And I'd like to know, anyway, how did that girl happen to leave her pants in your room?"

Facts are like boats floating on an ocean of feeling. . . .

Ignoring

The relationship in which one partner ignores the loving other is the deadliest. The message is: "As far as I am concerned you are dead." It is psycho-emotional *murder*.

In fact, for the loving partner it is as though, in a single stroke, death had dealt a double blow: to him and the beloved as well. The self-esteem of a person so hurt is drastically lowered. Courage and honesty are needed in order to accept the situation without wanting, unconsciously or purposely, to injure himself and possibly others. Surviving such a wound requires a great effort. Yet surviving is not enough! When at the pit of despair, who wants just to survive? The only solution is to soar as high as one is low.

Here are the directions for this recipe:

> *Accept the fact that you are at the pit of desolation, humiliation, loneliness.*
>
> *Practice "Had You Known How to Suffer . . ."*
>
> *Become aware of the danger of blocking off your feelings.*
>
> *When we are hurt we sometimes have the unconscious drive to pass our hurt on to others. Become aware of this possibility.*

Notice every time you might have the temptation to pass on your pain.

This requires tremendous vigilance, for such a temptation will be very subtly camouflaged and brilliantly rationalized.

Every time you catch this temptation perform these immediate almost simultaneous actions:

> Acknowledge the origin of the temptation.

> Acknowledge your pain.

> Instantaneously transform *it* into a useful or beautiful action, word, thought—soar as high as you are low. *BE THE MAGIC TRANSFORMER!*

Slave and Master: Identity Lost and Repossessed

The kind of relationship in which one person lives and communicates with the other only as long as that other is a useful, obedient slave can exist only between two people who have been deeply hurt by life. The person who wants to revenge himself by making a slave of his companion must have been hurt, frustrated and humiliated. And what about the partner who accepts his role as slave? What amount of terror is accumulated in this person's unconscious? Before such a situation can be improved, both partners must acknowledge their distorted relationship and decide to either dissolve or change it.

Lincoln said that he didn't want to be a slave—but neither did he want to be a master. In the slave-master relationship, each depends on the other. "Man lives asleep in a nightmare of unfulfilled desires," is a Sufi saying which characterizes the life of two persons whose love and hatred is so interfused as to be somewhat indistinguishable.

And what are these persons' unfulfilled desires? In extreme cases the motivating desires are deeply subconscious —images possibly imprinted during prenatal periods, at birth or in early infancy.

The self-image of inferiority and impotence of a person

who wants to subjugate another human being must be so invasive that it needs continuously to be denied. The exercise of power over anyone who will accept it gives provisional satisfaction to that need.

The unfulfilled desires of the accepting slave might also have roots in traumas suffered in the womb (when the very existence of the tiny being was, or felt, threatened), or during birth (when existence often is threatened). To assuage the unconscious terror of nonexistence, anything is acceptable, including slavery under a master who is rarely loved, often feared and despised.

At times love is part of this unwholesome relationship, but the main motivations for master and slave to stay together are a need to suffer and impose suffering; a terror of being alone; possibly a fear of dying alone.

A recipe for this tragic human bondage? First, there must be recognition and acknowledgment of the situation. Whether only one or both partners decide to change the relationship, practice "Be Your Own Ideal Parents" and "Mystery Suspended among Infinities." Follow with "Identity Lost and Repossessed."

IDENTITY LOST AND REPOSSESSED
We have many possibilities within us. We are not just one person, we are a legion! If you are locked into a slave-master relationship, it is partly because you permit one aspect of yourself—in this case the aspect of being a slave or a master—to take up most of your energy and color your life.

Directions:

> Reflect on the fact that you are not just a slave or a slave driver. Realize that situations, feelings, states of mind

and body have, rationally or irrationally, made you act as though being a slave or a master is your only identity, your only possible way to live and to be.

Decide that you are going to weaken, by all the means at your disposal, this unwanted identity.

Decide that you are going to give energy and attention to a completely different aspect of yourself. You are going to repossess your forgotten identity.

Look into yourself for this forgotten identity.

Think and relive times in your life when you did not act as a slave or a master.

Look into activities—work or play—in which you participated and felt happy and comfortable.

Relive a situation in which you were not preoccupied by winning or losing but in which you felt as if you were in your own unique place, doing your own unique thing, in harmony with yourself and your environment—feel the identity involved in that.

Feel the distance between this identity and the slave-master identity.

Remember those times, those moments, when the slave-master identity was not part of you, when you were light and fresh and free, unpossessed and unpossessing. Breathe deeply of that freshness, which will dissolve the ugly dream of slave and master. As you breathe, close your eyes and feel your forgotten identity becoming more and more alive, more and more real. It is there, it is you! It may need some nourishing; like a neglected plant needs sun, this part of you needs the warmth of your loving attention. If your eyes moisten when you realize your neglect for this creative, sensitive part of yourself, let those tears be a vitalizing water that brings your plant back to life. Feel this forgotten identity with all the intense reality of which you are capable. Close your eyes and direct fresh energy to your repossessed identity. It might have had a different name from your present one; or you may want to give it one.

With eyes still closed, stretch your body, move around.

Then take a posture that characterizes the repossessed identity that you are bringing back to life.

Open your eyes and hold on your face the expression of that identity.

Hold posture and expression for three or four minutes.

Repeat this three times a day.

Decide on one activity (work or play) which is going to involve your repossessed identity. Indulge in it as much as possible. It may even be a new career or a new relationship.

Do not feel that this recipe is asking too much of you. What *is* asking too much of you is your slave-master relationship. Its solution is similar to that of this riddle: "How do you clear a glass of turbid water without emptying the glass?"

Think about the answer. Whether you find it or not, turn this book upside down, and read.

Answer: By pouring clear water into the glass full of turbid water. Gradually the clear water will displace the turbid water. Similarly, by pouring the clear energy of your repossessed identity into the turbid one, you actualize the desired transformation in yourself.

*If in doubt about the motive of a criticism, ask yourself
these questions:*

What is the emotion inspiring this criticism?

    Frustration

    Affection

    Interest

    Lack of love

    Self-doubt

    Misunderstanding

    A sense of duty

    Necessity

    A longing for perfection

    Love

*What is the emotion with which this criticism is re-
ceived?*

    Fear

    Love

    Openness

    Resentment

    Frustration

    Gratefulness

    Interest

    Anxiety

    Sense of inferiority

Vendetta

Another type of relationship is that of two people whose life together is, in part, a self-perpetuating vendetta. Vendetta is such a dramatic word that we would probably be shocked to think that sometimes we act revengefully toward a person dear to us. But think a moment: even good relationships are not completely free of discord. When frustration reaches our resistance level, it is human to react negatively. It *is* human, but neither beneficial nor intelligent. Moreover, why not *act* instead of react? Experience the freedom of initiating an action, rather than becoming a link in a negative chain reaction! This negative chain reaction, vendetta, is carried on through several generations in some countries—years after the original offender is dead. The offense may also be distorted or forgotten, but the traditionally imposed obligation to avenge is kept alive by misplaced family pride. Fortunately, we are not the victims of this type of slavery in our culture.

In personal relationships vendettas occur mostly on a subconscious level. Can you remember as a child the feeling of being punished unjustly? And soon after, unexpectedly doing something wrong—failing in school, breaking a dish, being mean to a passer-by . . . ?*

* This concept is developed in *You Are Not the Target*, Laura Huxley.

Unclarified childhood resentments can continue into adulthood. For example: a husband may address his wife in a manner which has a slight resemblance to the way she was spoken to by her father. Even the use of a similar endearing phrase can trigger in the wife a whole series of emotions which make her behave toward the husband as if he were that other man, her father. The husband may also have some unfinished relationship and react to the wife's attack accordingly. When involved in a stressful relationship it is a good idea to reflect upon whether we are acting out a vendetta. A wife might, because of financial or other unaccepted restriction by a husband, revenge herself by withholding tenderness and sexual pleasure. The husband might in turn decide to find it somewhere else. It is lack of honest communication that worsens such situations. If the financial restriction of the husband had been adequately understood and agreed upon, a useless, long chain of suffering would have been avoided.

It takes considerable courage for a couple to recognize that their problem may originate in a hidden or open need for revenge. If this possibility is admitted, a great step toward a solution is accomplished. As with all problems concerning relationships, we suggest that each person experience separately the recipe "Be Your Own Ideal Parents" and "Mystery Suspended among Infinities."

After both partners have experienced these recipes several times, and if both agree to work on the relationship, do the following together.

> Each of you, in turn, is a sculptor. Your clay is the body of your partner.
>
> Pose your bodies to make statues expressing the following:
>
> This is the way you make me feel (Mary puts

John's body in the position expressing the way he makes her feel).

This is the way I wish to make you feel (John puts Mary's body in the position he would like to make her feel).

Then reverse the roles.

Experiencing in this way what you do to each other will open the door of understanding.

When you are the sculptor be attentive to mold details: mouth, eyebrows, hair, etc.

When you are the statue cooperate fully with the sculptor.

If, when someone close to you admires or praises another person, you feel covertly criticized, beware! You are going into a tormented daydream. Interrupt it on the spot: ask instantly and candidly: "Is your praising of _____ meant as a criticism of me?"

Possessiveness

A wife has a clear view of how her husband *should* be to fulfill her life—what his work *should* be—and how he *should* do it—which employer or secretary he *should* have —what he *should* eat, drink, say, etc.

A husband knows exactly what his wife *should* wear— the friends she *should* have—the books she *should* read.

The invasion of the physical, emotional and mental space of another person is a widespread situation not limited to the wife-husband relationship. To possess and/ or to allow oneself to be possessed in such a manner is un-ethical and insidiously destructive. If both partners realize the situation and decide to change it, practicing the follow-ing recipes will speed the change. The solution is more laborious if only one partner wants to modify the relation-ship. However, no relationship can remain exactly the same if there is a transformation in one of the partners. Often the reluctant partner is either induced or inspired to take stock of his or her behavior as a result of the other's change in attitude. Change is effective: preaching or push-ing generally brings about a contrary reaction.

Even when living in a large house where physical space is available, a couple stuck in a possessive relationship often invade each other's privacy. Whether or not physical space is available, it is necessary to create our own psycho-emotional space.

Directions:

Make a total decision: "I am creating my own space into which _____ cannot enter unless I consciously and lovingly let him enter. This space which I create will clarify our relationship and give me strength to change it." Unless you take this decision with complete organismic honesty, do not read further.

Realize that this invisible space can be as real as a brick.

Realize that you have probably done this before in an unconscious, possibly negative way. You might have been told you were difficult to communicate with, or aloof or cold. You had made a space around you, maybe unwillingly, and people felt it. This is an automatic and unconscious act which often has negative consequences. We want a conscious action producing a conscious space.

Find five minutes three times a day to be alone.

Permit nothing to interrupt these five-minute periods.

Close your eyes and stand relaxed, but not slumped. Align your body totally perpendicular to the earth: feet about twelve inches apart and parallel to each other; arms and hands loose; head easily poised on top of your straight, unbent spine.

Now become aware of your skin—scan every inch of your skin.

Now scan your skin again, but let your awareness dwell on the inner part of your skin.

Now feel an essence oozing from the inner part of your skin like a fragrance from a flower. This essence is seeping through every pore of your skin, surrounding you with a unique space which extends several inches from your body.

Do not move from your initial position. Totally attentive to the essence exuding from and enveloping you, you feel its inviolable, invisible protection. You feel strong and secure in it, for only invited guests can enter your space.

After the five-minute period let go of your space.

As you become familiar with your space you will be able to create it in an instant when you wish protection from a person or a vibration. Pause a second, feel the inner part of your skin, the essence oozing out and forming your protective space.

Be sure to use this recipe *only* when you wish to protect yourself. Don't let your space become a permanent unmovable structure around you. Like a space suit, put it on only when you are in an atmosphere in which it would be difficult to breathe freely.

Silent One-Candle Dinner

At times a relationship with a dear one becomes muddy. We know there are some precious jewels in the mud but the harder we look the less we succeed in finding them. We have followed the advice of counselors, we may have had open encounters to air out our complaints according to the best psychological rules. We looked into each other's eyes . . . these methods may have helped, and yet where are those jewels? You may find them again, without looking, if the two of you have a "Silent One-Candle Dinner."

Directions:

You have agreed to have a silent one-candle dinner.

Then—

Choose a place and time where you know there will be silence and absolutely no interruption from the telephone, visitors, etc. Be very careful in the choice of food. Have one course only, but one that's pleasing to both of you. It would be just as disturbing for a meat-and-potatoes man to be presented with a few sticks of celery, carrots and some mock turkey meat as it would for a vegetarian to be presented with a piece of a dead animal —with or without candle!

The preparation of the food is important—even if you decide on something as simple as bread and cheese, wine and fruits. The attitude when choosing and arranging these foods is important.

Play with this little recipe—make it your own. Decide whether you prepare this dinner together or each a part of it, or one the entire meal.

Choose a dish which is complete so you needn't get up from the table. It is all there.

Turn off the lights, sit facing each other and place the candle between you.

Each of you takes a match: one lights his or her match and with it the match of the other partner. Then light the candle together.

Chew the first mouthful as Aldous describes it in Island:

> "In Pala," she explained, "we don't say grace before meals. We say it with meals. Or rather we don't say grace; we chew it."
> "Chew it?"
> "Grace is the first mouthful of each course—chewed and chewed until there's nothing left of it. And all the time you're chewing you pay attention to the flavour of the food, to its consistency and temperature, to the pressures on your teeth and the feel of the muscles in your jaws."
> "And meanwhile, I suppose, you give thanks to the Enlightened One, or Shiva, or whoever it may be?"
> Shanta shook her head emphatically. "That would distract your attention, and attention is the whole point. Attention to the experience of something given, something you haven't invented. Not the memory of a form of words addressed to somebody in your imagination."

After that first long chewing continue eating in silence. There may be mounting tension. Fine.

Release of emotion, tears, laughter, may emerge in either one or both of you. On this occasion, just accept what emerges, joy or pain, good or bad, in you or in the other, and do it respectfully without interruption or comment.

Accept, don't judge, above all don't talk.

Don't put a limit of time to your "Silent One-Candle Dinner." Let it unfold. You might, in a few hours, relive and review silently a relationship of years. Let it happen: its beginning, its development, its various ups and downs.

This silent one-candle dinner may be the end of the relationship or it may be its blossoming.

You may even find that the relationship never was.

Or that it is just now being born.

Be a Birth Giver: A Recipe to Improve Any Relationship

Lord, let me not judge a man until I have walked two moons in his moccasins.
—Navajo prayer

How unfair it is to judge at a distance, to judge only with our intellect, without experiencing the other being, without at least trying to walk in his shoes. This recipe is an extension and a deepening of "Jump in the Other's Place," a recipe from *You Are Not the Target*. The two can be done separately; but if done together they enhance one another. Both recipes have clarified, ameliorated and at times even resolved difficulties in a relationship.

Understanding is often magic. Its absence causes irritation, impedes communication, blocks energies. Its presence is creative. Understanding is a birth giver. We often speak of "human potentials." Understanding is a way to actualize those potentials. If nobody sees them, if nobody understands them, they will remain potentials; only when they are recognized can they develop.

Think of some particular time in your life during which

you were understood, when interest and attention were directed toward you, and your whole being was granted the right to be what it was. Relive your feeling at that time, and what happened within you. Probably something was given birth in you. *Stop reading, and take time to relive that event.*

Now relive a time when attention was *not* given to you. You wanted to talk to somebody, but no one listened. You hoped that someone would give you his attention, but everyone was too busy. You thought that someone had grasped what you had said, only to see later that you were totally misinterpreted. Ignoring is not just neutral. You are affected by another person's unawareness. It can be a death giver.

It is often not in our power to elicit understanding from another. It *is* in our power to decide whether we want to be birth givers or death givers.

If you decide to be a birth giver, use this recipe for that purpose.

> *Choose a person who is quite close to you. You are going to understand the universe of that person.*
>
> *Imagine being that person, and imaginatively live his day. Imagine being him, when you wake up in the morning, in his room.*
>
> *Imagine how it feels to have a body like that person has.*
>
> *See his room from his point of view.*
>
> *Wear his clothing.*
>
> *Go to work using the transportation he uses.*
>
> *Imagine his success and failure in his occupation, the people he relates to, their impact on him.*
>
> *Imagine his life during those work hours.*

See the world with his eyes. Project yourself into each hour of his day.

Imagine his trip back home; the impact the day has had on him; how his body feels.

Imagine what he hopes to find when he returns home.

What did we do wrong?

Thousands of parents lay awake at night asking that question as the increasing wave of mental disturbance, suicide and delinquency among the young baffles and destroys.

What did we do wrong?

We had wanted John so much and he was so special, so tender, so loving. My husband worked twice as hard so I didn't have to hold a job when Johnny was a little boy. We sent him to the best school. We took him camping, welcomed his friends. When he started to get in trouble, we sent him into therapy; he has been going to a therapist off and on for five years, and yesterday he was arrested for the fourth time. We are broken financially and in every way . . .

What did we do wrong?

She is sixteen, beautiful, intelligent and loved, although she doesn't think so. She has run away from six schools: there has been promiscuity, drugs, stealing. She is full

*of hate for us; when she attempted suicide, it was difficult
not to do the same.*

What did we do wrong?

*With some variation, these reports are multiplied by the
thousands throughout the nation. The diagnoses of these
tragic events are numerous and brilliant; the remedies are
numerous and brilliant; the resulting "cures" (aside from
the healing factor of time with its own remedies) are scant
and uncertain.*

*Often in spite of loving parents, who provide good en-
vironment, school, psychotherapy, etc., a young person
may be depressed, neurotic and even delinquent. If the
intake of certain foods, vitamins, minerals and enzymes
is modified, these symptoms often diminish drastically, even
disappear.*

(See information in "Appendix One: Project Sanity.")

We Are All Magicians

No change can take place in a relationship until the persons involved change their images of each other. It is a natural function of the mind to create and project images. In a relationship we create in our mind the image of the other person just as we take a photograph. This photograph, however, is more than visual; it comprises all sensations—smell, touch, sound, motion plus psycho-emotional and physical emanations. It is a complex picture, for it is a composite of the subject's qualities and our interpretation of them. Then we add another power to the image: *the label!*

> "She is lazy."
> "He is a liar."
> "They are a hopeless bunch of teen-agers."

The label vitalizes the image and creates expectation. The following is an example of what expectation created by an image can do:

> . . . the children at South San Francisco's Spruce Elementary School were given IQ tests. Teachers were falsely told that the test would show which pupils were to "spurt ahead" academically. They were given

the names of 20 per cent of the student body, ran-
domly selected from all grades and all three achieve-
ment tracks, and were told that every pupil listed
would improve dramatically within a year.

Almost as if by magic [my emphasis], each of those
pupils listed made the predicted dramatic gains, while
the rest of the student body did not. Only the teachers
—not the pupils or parents—were given the predictions. . . . A year later, when all the children were
retested, the "spurters" showed an average IQ gain of
12.2 points, compared with 8.42 for a control group
representing the rest of the student body.*

"Almost as if by magic" is correct: magic is based on
feeling, thought and expectation vitalizing a clear and detailed image. In his anthropological research on primitive societies Bronislaw Malinowski reports the unfailing
power of the warlock's self-fulfilling prophecy. A warlock
spreads the news among the tribe that a certain individual
is to die within twenty-four hours. In this way he creates
the environment of expectation. Then he focuses his attention (or "points the bone") in the direction of his victim
and imagines his becoming violently ill and dying. The
person generally dies within twenty-four hours. This
ought to make us reflect on the extent to which doctors'
diagnostic predictions are self-fulfilling prophecies.

We can see then that we are all magicians: it is up to us
to choose whether to be a white or gray or black magician!

The following directions will improve a relationship by
changing a negative image and its projection into either a
neutral or beneficial one—in other words, they will show
us how to train ourselves in white magic.

---

* *Teaching General Semantics,* edited by Mary S. Morian. International
Society for General Semantics, San Francisco, 1969.

Choose a relationship which you wish to improve.

Three times a day, for five minutes, sit quietly and think of your image of the person involved. Many of the undesirable characteristics which are making your relationship difficult will hurl themselves at you as you contemplate your image of the person. Do not judge yourself, the image or the other person—just observe the antics of all three as if you were observing a show totally detached from you. If emotion arises, then observe the arising emotion. By withholding vitality from the undesirable traits, you will weaken their power over you, and, in all probability, their power over the other person. These undesirable traits, like little devils, will spring upon you, doing their best to ensnare you in their dance—don't participate in it; non-participation and non-repression are of the essence.

At the end of each ten-minute period, flash quickly and intensely on one of the other person's characteristics which is valuable and pleasing to you. This contemplation is short but so vivid and powerful that you will feel you also possess that valuable characteristic. Hold it for a few seconds, and let that be the closing of this recipe.

Conclusion: Pastime Games

Paola F., a bright Italian teen-ager, was trying to improve a relationship between two people in her family. She wrote me: ". . . and then, after you have tried everything and nothing works, the only thing to do is to be as kind as possible to everyone."

The "Pastime Games" which follow are inspired by that thought.

> Buildings, skeletons, flowers, walls, bridges, mountains—any structure is given relevance by the empty space surrounding it. Pause gives space to music. So it is with our TIME: between the states of "being busy" there are empty spaces. Sometimes this emptiness is heavenly; other times, we may not be in a frame of mind to enjoy it. Then we can make those little spaces lively and significant with these pastime games.

WHEN ADMIRED . . .

we become admirable:

> Admiration is sometimes magic, but beware of giving routine admiration or flattery, automatic pseudo-polite compliments. Admire those characteristics which are still in the early budding state. Recognize the quality that the person would like to develop: communicate with that person as though that quality were already there. But, be light! *Misplaced abundance of admiration could have the same result as overwatering a budding plant—it may drown it.*

BODY PENCIL

When you want to send a silent, loving word to a person present or distant:

> Stand up straight; feet parallel about two or three inches apart; fingers, hands, shoulders relaxed.
>
> Imagine you are a long straight pencil—its point reaches to heaven.
>
> Write that loving word or phrase with your whole body pencil on heaven: it will take care of communicating the message.

LADY BOUNTIFUL

Let any one of your friends, enemies, relatives, acquaintances, impersonal contacts (telephone operators, clerks, etc.) pass through your mind. Keep him in your consciousness for a short time and project to him a strong, beautiful vibration. This can be color—heavenly blue, rosy, golden, white. Or the vibration can be imagined as a pleasant sound, a word, an image or a pure thought.

Don't take this too seriously—just have fun with it like Farquhar's Lady Bountiful distributing gifts that are immediately and magically replaced with greater gifts. You can continue this game with people you have heard about but do not know; with people living or dead, in your past or in your future; with some stranger, whom you may meet tomorrow or ten years from now, or never!

Do this while waiting at the dentist's office or in line for some boring chore, when sleep doesn't come, or anytime. For one month experiment with it for five or ten minutes out of the 1440 minutes in a day. Indulge in this pastime: it may become your favorite! Should these vibrations not reach their destination, they will still boomerang back to you.

COY LIGHT

Think of having a little light a few inches above your head—just like a hat that does not touch your head or ruffle your hair. It goes with you everywhere you go—stays with you whether you are happy or sad, asleep or awake, busy or idle, sick or healthy. This light is often as timid as a violet; at times it is almost self-effacing. Generally, it does not flash itself around as lights often do, saying: "Look at me! How modest I am! I am a little light." But it is a few inches above your head—all the time.

You may remember that in You Are Not the Target we discovered a sunflower in the center of you and everyone else. The same with this little light: it is always there, a few inches above your head and everyone's head. Earthly sunflowers in the middle and heavenly lights over the top. You fill your world with mirthful, enchanting in-habitants—they enjoy it as much as you do!

Try this when you speak to someone: look at that light over the top of his head. Even if it happens to be one of those days when the light plays its violet game and is self-effacing, look at it just the same. You will see how this person's posture becomes more beautiful, more secure—it will straighten and lengthen from inside, almost without movement and without your saying anything about it.

Part Four

We all play:
children with toys,
grownups with a toy called making sense.

DEFEATED FROM THE BEGINNING

Tantalized by rationalization, enchanted by righteousness, we are defeated from the beginning if we try to apply our logic to an apparently non-logical universe. The rain falls and the sun shines on the just and the unjust. An amoeba cannot apprehend a human being, and neither can we, at this time, apprehend the universal symphony. We can only accept it and attempt to play in tune with the mysterious, immense orchestra whose instruments are largely unknown to us; whose unpredictable conductor has infinite inventiveness, boundless power, harmonies and rhythms inconceivable to us.

It is an enticing and noble pastime to stretch our intellectual muscles and strive to apologize for infinite absurdity, to explain eternal bliss as organized religions attempt to do.

For those not attuned to the church's explanatory revelation, this is an alternative solution: let go of the stressful need to explain and apologize for pain, sickness and death. Focus instead on the undaunted eyes of:

The will to Good
and
The will to Beauty

Suggested direction:

> Today I will not eat or drink or sleep unless I have done something good or beautiful.

When you feel like insulting someone write the wounding word on your palate with your tongue. Then decide whether the insulting word would benefit anyone.

YOUR EVER-RECEPTIVE
CONFIDANT

It won't take long before we talk to our plants (whether a huge tree or a little pot) as we talk to our pets. Science has established that plants know and respond to our thoughts and emotions.* This fact is as ancient as creation, for our cells and the cells of plants have much in common in origin and structure. What is new is that science is able to measure this fact in terms acceptable to our intellect. It is curious how reassured we are when scientific instruments confirm our intuitive knowledge.

No matter how busy or poor one is, it is always possible to have a growing plant. A potato, carrot, beet or onion kept in water gives forth foliage just as lively as that of an expensive plant.

You can communicate anything to your plant, but it responds particularly well to your good feelings: tell it all the good things about yourself which you wouldn't feel comfortable saying to others. Even on dark days, when you have some difficulty in finding things you like about yourself, find at least one good thing to tell your plant. Describe to your plant, not just once but many times, the

* *The Secret Life of Plants,* Peter Tompkins and Christopher Bird. Harper & Row, 1973.

ideal picture of yourself. Of course this ideal picture is within you, or you would not be able to imagine and describe it. It is like a seed which contains leaves and flowers and fruits—a whole tree. Your plant understands all this very well. You confide to your plant the special qualities contained in your unique seed—living, growing, sprouting —qualities within you, still too faint to be seen by human beings, but easily detected by your plant.

The two of you dwell on these qualities. Your plant will show its appreciation for your trust and will bloom for you. Just as food and water were not enough for you when you were an infant—and even now—they are not enough for your plant. It wants your trust, your admiration, your protection.

Remember that your ever-receptive confidant is defenseless and totally at your mercy, just as you were at the mercy of your parents as an infant. On a gloomy day you may feel that your parents did not realize how defenseless you really were, how much attention and love you really needed in addition to food. The behavior of those mindless giants made you feel unwanted, unloved—made you feel as though *no place* was *your place*. Some of the child's feelings may be left over in the adult if he feels that never, never is he in his *own right and unique place*. Tell your plant that *it* is in its own right place because you love it there; that you are going to see to its comfort, and give it your attention.

Soon your plant will identify with you. All the good and beautiful thoughts, feelings and actions that involve you will be reflected in your ever-receptive confidant. Realize that it longs for your reassurance, attention and love just as you did, as we all do, especially when we are new and helpless.

Speak to your plant and to the little child that may be

still within you as you would to a lovable, defenseless creature. No loneliness, no bitterness in this gentle space of child and plant. You are the guardian angel of both. Although you demand nothing, you are given an enormous reward: as the plant flourishes the child grows and its fear and loneliness are transformed into quiet and secure strength. As the past debris of the compost heap becomes nourishment for a new crop, so your past pain becomes nourishment for this new love—this love for yourself and your ever-receptive confidant.

No matter what your mood is, be sure to end your conversation with your ever-receptive confidant with an uplifting note. The plant cannot move around or go out and think of something else; it is going to stay where you leave it until you come back. Don't leave it in a downcast mood. Leave it with a bright image to respond to during your absence.

When Homo Erectus dared to make use of the destroying force of fire as creative energy to broaden his life and consciousness, he fostered his emergence into Homo Sapiens.

On a higher turn of the evolutionary spiral, Homo Sapiens is confronted with the same challenge, given the same opportunity: to transform the destructive power of toxic emotions into a fire of purification, and by widening his consciousness, to foster his emergence into Homo Divinus.

In this Age of Audacity are we as daring as Homo Erectus was 800,000 years ago?

NOW I WANT TO DO
PROPELLERS: EXPRESS SERIES

"Propellers" is a name given a pen exercise in the practice of Grapho-Therapeutics.* It looks like this:

and is designed to facilitate fluency and control of the whole personality through the action of writing.

A little girl was asked to do a page of this exercise. She was unwilling but complied for a while. She had only a little more space to fill when she stopped. The teacher insisted that she continue. "If I finish the page," asked the little girl, "may I then spit on my propellers?" The teacher agreed. Quickly the little girl finished the page of propellers, and just as quickly, she spat on them. Then immediately, with a brisk, happy tone, she said: "Now I *want* to do propellers!"

* *Grapho-Therapeutics: Pen and Pencil Therapy,* Paul de Sainte Colombe. Popular Library, 1973.

This little episode was for me a beautiful lesson in creative education. How often is a teacher exacting, yet receptive to a student's feelings? How often does a teacher foster an open and *harmless* expression of the student's frustration?

The reaction of a less-enlightened teacher might have been:

"No spitting in my classroom!" (High-pitched querulous voice.)

"Now be a nice little girl, finish your exercise." (Saccharine-sweet voice.)

"Well, if you don't feel like doing it, let's stop." (Tired, depressed voice.)

These reactions would have stimulated only (1) resentment, (2) a stereotyped false image or (3) undisciplined laissez-faire. Among the features that could make for a good school, in my opinion, a prominent one would be to give students—in the morning before starting the day, and in the afternoon before going home—the psychophysical means to release *consciously* and harmlessly the negative feelings accumulated at home before arriving at school, and in school before going home. This should be done with the approval of parents and teachers, and what a blessing it would be for them! Then they too could release their own toxic feelings accumulated during the day. Dinner would taste better and be more nourishing on all levels.

It gives us support and self-esteem to know that our uncomfortable, at times painful, toxic feelings are not looked down upon, but are simply considered something from which to be released—something to wash up, just as we wash our hands. The feeling-tone of the little girl was transformed in a few seconds when she could openly, with her teacher's approval, express her annoyance. Intelligent support and, *when harmlessly done,* freedom of expression, are as necessary to our well-being as the air we breathe.

In the following "Express Series" we suggest a few recipes to give conscious expression to our constricting, unwanted feelings, in ways that are harmless and effective. In addition to these, you may find your own original way to spit on your propellers!

Express Series

The following series of twelve mini-recipes is designed to relieve unspecified inner tensions and pressures to which we give various names: anxiety, fear, boredom, exhaustion, rage, pain, sadness. Regardless of the name, we feel better immediately and avoid future troubles if we release and transform these stressful pressures *consciously*.

The recipes in this series take only a few minutes.

We wash our body every day—but how can we be and feel clean if our emotional and psychological essence is not similarly cleansed every day?

This cleaning involves the use of muscles. Albert Szent-Györgyi, twice Nobel prize winner, who has researched the nature of muscles for twenty years, wrote:

> Muscles are the seat of the most violent and massive energy transformation.

United to imagination and directed by will this conscious muscular transformation of energy is one of the most wondrous and always available means to prevent illness and to clear our heart and mind.

EXPRESS ONE

Arms open, stand in a doorway and push the frame on both sides with all your strength, as though to widen the space. As you push the frame, you push that unpleasant feeling away, open your chest and let your breathing widen and deepen.

EXPRESS TWO

Shout those words charged with feelings which you have repressed all day, all year, all life. Take care to shout only in a place where you cannot be heard—where your shouting will not boomerang destructively upon you. One safe place may be your car, all windows closed.

EXPRESS THREE
If you are confused:

> *Blow several times, as hard as you can.*
>
> *Blow confusion away.*
>
> Clench your fists, concentrate all energy to the top of your mouth. Make a small opening with your lips and with great intensity, blow a stream of air concentrated like a laser beam. Your concentrated breath is very powerful, and it blows confusion out and away; but you must put into it all your energy and your conviction—otherwise, the confusion will remain there, and any adverse wind might blow it back at you.

EXPRESS FOUR
When angry, improve your arms:

> Close your fists as tightly as possible, squeeze as hard as you can.
>
> Put your toxic feeling in one fist and tighten still more.
>
> Relax.
>
> Now bring your imagination into play.
>
> Make a hideous object representing your toxic feeling, and squeeze that imaginary object until you destroy it.
>
> Destroy it so you will not harm yourself or the person who stimulated the toxic feeling.

EXPRESS FIVE

Jump up and down like a child having a tantrum. Let your arms swing wildly and scream NO NO NO.

Variation:

Do this with a partner. Face each other and outscream, outjump, out-NO each other!

EXPRESS SIX

Place your feet about three or four feet from a wall, put your hands on the wall, and inhale as you get ready to push.

Now with your entire body leaning on the hands, PUSH the wall, and while bending your elbows until your forehead touches the wall, exhale all the words you wanted to say, but didn't. Exhale by making a very thin, small opening with your lips.

Push and exhale until you are completely empty. Remain empty in the ending position, then inhale while your body straightens up. Hands and feet don't move.

Repeat at least five times.

EXPRESS SEVEN

When you feel that you are getting out of shape:

> *Jump the rope.*
>
> *The rope may be real or imagined.*
>
> *Jump again, but this time imagine that the rope makes an oval of fire around you.*

EXPRESS EIGHT

When you want to get rid of some toxic memories:

> *Make a movement as if to throw something out the window.*
>
> *Perform this movement with as much strength as you can.*
>
> *Now visualize the toxic memory you want to do away with.*
>
> *It might look like some squishy thing, or like a big brown stone.*
>
> *Divide it into ten pieces.*
>
> *Open the window, take one piece at a time, and throw it as far as possible.*

EXPRESS NINE

Take an old telephone directory (*it is a good idea to save them*).

On one page, with a hard pen or pencil:

Write one word that bothers upsets confuses you.

Draw a face that bothers upsets confuses you.

Draw an object that bothers upsets confuses you.

Tear off this page—make a ball of it—throw it in the air —play with it—throw it to the dog—burn it—put it in the garbage . . .

Again and again repeat steps two and three, until you feel relieved of the toxicity stimulated by that word face object—even if it takes a megalopolis telephone directory.

EXPRESS TEN

When you feel you need protection:

> *Make a sound.*
>
> *Hum it.*
>
> *Hum until you find the sound which is really your own.*
>
> *Now keep humming it, and imagine that it is creating a vibratory field all around you.*
>
> *This vibratory field is of your favorite color and IS light and energy.*

EXPRESS ELEVEN

After you have had an unpleasant conversation, meeting, letter, etc.:

> Shake your hands and arms and back several times energetically. Now do the same, but imagine that they are covered with sticky mud, and you want to get rid of it. Each time you shake, some of the mud is thrown away. Shake hands and arms really hard! and harder! and harder!

> Do the same with your legs: stand on one and shake the mud from the other. First shake the calf joint, then the knee joint, then swing the entire leg from the hip, shaking off whatever is still left of sticky toxicity.

EXPRESS TWELVE
When disgruntled:

> *Ask not how many gifts life refuses you, but how many you are able to accept.*

FROM ANOTHER PLANET

Do you have some overflowing drawers, boxes or closets whose contents you intend to sort and clean and possibly throw away? The most important container to sort and clean and empty is our consciousness—the container of our thoughts, our feelings, our life.

We are going to observe the content of our consciousness. When we do this we do not decide what to keep or what to throw away: this will take us into the land of decision-making, which involves judgment and action. In this recipe simply *observe* what goes on in your consciousness—if you are surprised or shocked about what you find there, observe your surprise and your shock. You may find angry beasts and wounded angels, decaying corpses and budding roses, chattering bores and poetic sounds, bottomless shabbiness, glittering peaks. Don't qualify (as I have just done) the content of your container; just let it pass before you without expressing opinions, qualifications, preferences, as though you were looking at it from another planet.

Directions:

Take a few minutes before beginning to observe what goes on inside of you–OBSERVE IT FROM AN-OTHER PLANET.

Close your eyes and transport yourself to this new planet in your own way.

When you arrive make yourself comfortable and look at planet Earth.

You need a telescope to look down to Earth. Even through the telescope what you see is small and sooth-ingly distant.

Sitting on your private planet, you look at yourself through your telescope and observe the content of your consciousness.

The most vital things in your life are there–dramas, pains, pleasures.

From this planet you observe the show that you see on the lens of your telescope. This show is the content of your consciousness. Look at it without opinions, reactions, preferences–certainly without attempting to change any-thing.

If you wish, you can put your telescope down and write a word or two. Without interrupting the "show" write just one word representing a whole sequence of thoughts, feelings, events that arise from your consciousness. Do not try to write it all out. For instance, a long grumbling series of words and thoughts may pass through your mind in regard to a complication in getting insurance money to pay for the fender of your car which was bent in an acci-dent that was not your fault; how long will the insurance company take to pay; what a pain in the neck etc. . . . etc. . . . If you wrote all this down you would be "sucked" into thinking about the action to be taken: buy another car, change insurance policies, etc. All you have to write, even with your eyes closed, is: "car" or "insurance" or "accident" or "fender," or whichever word comes first to you. A shorthand pad will do. Write the date before going to the chosen planet, or if you do this as we suggest for thirty days straight, just indicate the session's number.

Don't read what you wrote until the end of the thirty-day period.

After thirty days you will know quite a bit about the content of your consciousness—about how some of your energy is spent. If you actually see the content of your consciousness on paper, in words with a meaning only you understand, solutions and clarifications will emerge. You will see how, by honestly observing our inner world, changes can spontaneously occur.

After you are competent in this recipe, you may find this variation exhilarating:

Jump to still another planet and observe yourself sitting with the telescope observing the content of your consciousness on Earth. Leaping from planet to planet you will be observing yourself observing yourself.

Then return to Earth.

Having absorbed Heavenly Energies, you are lavishly pouring them forth here and now.

At times we are caught by recurring unpleasant moods, tediously claiming our attention like uninvited visitors. We have many recipes to express and transform such moods. But today, with the intrinsic authority of a great leader, simply dismiss your mood as an indiscreet solicitor.

LIKE A TIGER IN THE JUNGLE

In this recipe we speak of aloneness as the state of being physically alone with no qualification—and of loneliness as the suffering caused by the state of being alone, physically, emotionally, psychologically.

The purpose of this recipe is to enhance the capacity to *enjoy your own company.*

"I am lonely   I am lonely   I am lonely"

You hear it shouted, cried, whimpered, murmured, and at times the soundless sob is unbearable.

Why are you promiscuous? Because I am lonely.

Why do you overeat? Because I am lonely.

Why do you take drugs, alcohol, cigarettes? Because I am lonely.

Why do you buy all those silly gadgets you cannot afford and don't need? Because I am lonely.

This cry comes from every side.

But why did you marry him? Because I was lonely. Why do you live with her? Because a man gets lonely.

Loneliness, alas, seems to be the major motivation of many relationships—not friendship, or love, or mutuality of feeling, interests and ideals. No wonder there is such widespread disappointment in human relations.

Often a childhood fear is at the base of the fear of loneliness. Having been left alone as a child may remain in an adult as a feeling of intense discomfort, fear or terror.

It is not traumatic for a child to be left alone as long as he does not feel punished, and if he is fed and comfortable. In fact, it is necessary at times for a child to feel no other vibration around him and to get used to his own space. But often a child is left alone, sometimes in the dark, as punishment. When he grows up he forgets the punishment, but the state of *being alone* is associated with the feeling of *being wrong*.

Obscurely but powerfully, the adult feels that being alone diminishes him; it arouses in him discomfort, anxiety, restlessness. All kinds of fears emerge, the basic one being the fear of death. Being alone is often connected with the fear of death, which is sometimes confused with the fear of dying alone. If there is no underlying fear of death it is unlikely that there is any fear of being alone or of dying alone.

Many of us do not mind saying that we would not want to die alone, but in our culture, a fear of death is considered cowardice or weakness—it is not "manly." A culture imposes many unnecessary restraints on real feeling, and most of us accept these restraints. Being able to distinguish between those that are necessary and those that are harmful is an important part of the art of living.

There is a great difference between the natural desire for human companionship and the morbid state in which a person considers spending a few evenings or days alone a dread event. In an obscure way such a person has an all-pervasive fear which even casual company or entertainment can momentarily repress; but this fear and loneliness are only covered up and perpetuated. A lonely person does not often realize this situation and thus obsessively avoids being alone at any cost—at times the cost is high.

A good relationship naturally alleviates the feeling of loneliness, which may vanish altogether when there is trust and love. It is, however, easier to find good company when you can first enjoy your own. When a relationship is based on the inability to be alone, usually it becomes painful, sometimes tragic. An occupation based on one's capabilities, an inspiring quest and purpose, are also great dispellers of loneliness.

Loneliness can be caused by each, or none, or all of the reasons listed below—or by an infinite number of other causes not listed here.

Whichever the case, consider the following but don't spend much time in introspection.

I don't want to be alone and I feel lonely because:

My mother didn't love me.

My father, sister, grandmother, lover—in fact nobody ever loved me.

I may die if I am alone.

I don't want to die alone.

I am afraid of dying.

I have a feeling of darkness and suffocation which takes me back to my mother's womb—or to my birth.

I have no money.

I have money but it does not help me.

I want to be with another human being.

I don't like myself, so I am not good company for myself.

I eat food which disagrees with me, so my loneliness depends on my digestion.

Everything is so beautiful that I want to share it with someone.

I am in poor health.

The person I love died.

The person I love left me.

The person I love does not love me.

I stopped drinking.

I am getting old.

I am young and strong and those old fogies don't understand me.

It is raining.

I live in a big city.

I feel an intense absence.

(Add your own reasons. . . .)

These causes are all legitimate, true, important—as long as they feel real to you.

And now, whatever the cause of loneliness, realize that although it might have been or is produced partly by circumstances and people outside your control, the person who can do something about the here-now situation is *you*. This is the first and basic realization. The total acceptance of this feeling of loneliness includes the possibility of its changing. Accept the fact that something or someone in the past was not fair to you, but know that "it is only in the present that I can change the way the past influences me."

How can we change our relationship to the past? By living fully in the present. This is done by all the methods that sharpen awareness, described here and in other books. When your awareness is sharpened, widened, then your world is sharpened and widened. The world around us is immense. Surely some aspect of it merits your attention— just as you merit the attention of some aspect of the world around you. You will become aware of how many, many other people feel the same kind of loneliness you do, and you may be able to give them support.

And there is something else: a certain feeling of loneliness is basic to our nature. It is life's way to insure survival. For ever and since ever, two have longed to become one: the sperm looks for the ovum, and the ovum, as soon as it is made perfect by the union, begins to divide into billions of cells. This division creates a human being who, lonely, looks for some way to end that loneliness—to unite—with another human being, or with nature, art, or with that state of perfect oneness from which it initially came.

According to the Vedic doctrine, in the beginning there was blissful unity. Then unity felt the desire to express itself—so it did. So it does. It expresses itself in an infinite number of ways: planets, flowers, beasts, men, entities known and unknown. Each one is a spark of the original essence and yet a separated entity. Each one is possessed by a compelling need for a unique identity and yet longs for a reunion with the initial oneness, with Paradise Lost—and so the dance goes on. To the plaintive chant of loneliness, to the imperious rhythm of creativity, we dance—for ever and since ever—from ego-less oneness to lonesome separation. The greatest works of art, the truest loves, the shabbiest lives—all are directed by the eternal theme: one wanting to be two, two wanting to be one—loneliness is one of life's most powerful means of survival.

Directions:

>Accept the fact that loneliness is a part of life's process.
>
>Accept the fact that there is loneliness.
>
>Accept the fact that going to parties, talking incessantly, drinking, smoking, speeding, looking at TV for hours on end and similar activities, steal your life energy and only cover up your loneliness.

After you have gone through the previous directions, move ahead to these:

>Put aside half an hour out of the twenty-four hours to look at loneliness. Be sure there will be no disturbance or interruption during these periods. Use a timer so that you will know when the half hour is up.
>
>Sit comfortably, but not so comfortably that you might go to sleep (such a legitimate escape!). Observe what loneliness and fear of it does to you—the thoughts it brings, the actions it motivates, the relationships it compels you to have.
>
>This is not judging time—it is strictly observing time. Imagine that you are a cool scientist observing the subject of loneliness in relation to the subject of yourself.
>
>Now you are no longer a scientist: you are a Tiger. Silently, with the alertness that only survival inspires, like a Tiger in the jungle watching its prey, YOU WATCH! See what loneliness is trying to make you do today!

In our culture it is natural to ask: What will I get out of this? How much interest a year? How many pounds do I lose on this diet? How many miles per gallon? Only one person can honestly answer similar questions about the quality and the amount of benefit you will derive from experiencing the recipes. Only you *can answer—not by reading but by doing. Let your experience BE. Don't think or talk before doing the recipes, only afterwards.*

SEA-SKY PAINTING

I.

Sit comfortably erect.
As in the illustration, imagine that:

> Your face is duplicated on the back of your head. In other words, you have two identical faces, one on the front and one on the back side of your head. The only features which are not duplicated are your ears; they are located exactly between your two faces.

> Going through your head there are two thin poles. One comes out from the tips of your two noses and the other from the holes in your ears. These two thin poles cross right in the center of your head. At each end of these thin poles there is a bunch of bristles, forming four paint-brushes—two coming out of your ears, and two emerging from the tips of your two noses.

> You are on a very comfortable platform in the middle of the sea. There is only sea and sky around, below, above you. Your two faces see the same view.

> Become especially aware of the paintbrushes coming out of your noses.

> Keep your eyes closed throughout the recipe.

> These long paintbrushes are touching that place on the horizon where sea and sky meet.

With your two paintbrushes draw a line beginning at the horizon: By slowly moving your head upward, one line will go up in the sky while the other dips into the sea.

Visualize clearly the paintbrush going up in the sky while its opposite dips deep into the sea—

What color are you using?

Do you paint with the same color, back and front?

When your brushes emerge are they dripping?

Do your brushes emerge with the same color?

Notice how your sea-sky painting extends higher and higher into the sky, deeper and deeper into the sea.

Paint slowly; enjoy the sky and the sea, the colors and the progressively smoother feeling in your movements.

The golden ball bearings on which your neck moves are anointed with fragrant oil. It is your favorite fragrance. The longer and smoother your neck moves, the more you delight in the oil's fragrance.

Using the same directions, paint with the brushes that protrude from your ears. You are in the middle of the sea, therefore the landscape is the same: sky and sea, around, below, above you. Your neck moves your head toward and away from the top of your shoulders. Don't move the shoulder. One of your paintbrushes dips deep into the sea, while the other goes high into the sky. As in the previous sea-sky painting, colors, smoothness and fragrance are yours to create and enjoy.

Variations:

I expect you will invent several variations to this recipe. Here are a few—your neck will welcome them!

Using the four brushes simultaneously:

> Paint the number 8.
>
> Paint the letters of the alphabet.

Paint four wheels. With a little side movement (like Javanese dancers do), mark the center of the two wheels you have painted with the brushes coming out of your ears. With a little front-and-back movement of your neck, mark the center of the front and back wheels you have painted with the brushes coming out of your noses.

Now try this for relaxation:

Let go of the face on the back of your head and of the paintbrushes coming out of your ears. You have only one long paintbrush protruding from your nose. Write and paint in all colors on a distant wide, white wall:

your name

your portrait

the name of one you love

a secret message

a face you love

a landscape

a seascape

the most beautiful face you have ever seen

a high mountain

your inner universe

Paint how and where you intend to feel and be and look two years from now. Do this in great detail.

II. Sea-Sky Painting with Four Heads, Eight Faces and Sixteen Paintbrushes

One day when you feel in good contact with the triangle of Will, Imagination, Body, experience the following version of "Sea-Sky Painting." It requires good direction of imagination and an especially good control of your body, which must be kept motionless but very relaxed. You will appreciate this recipe much more after you have experienced it. To this version add all the preceding variations plus those your fantasy suggests.

Directions:

> In this sea-sky painting, you have four imaginary heads: each head has two faces and two double paintbrushes as in the first part of this recipe.

The location of your imaginary four heads is as follows:

Two heads in front of and three feet away from your shoulders in an upward oblique direction.

Two heads in back of and three feet away from your shoulders in an upward oblique direction.

If you were to raise your arm in an oblique upward way in front of you, you could almost touch your two front heads; if you put your arms up in back of you in an oblique way, you could almost touch your two back heads.

These four heads are like those in the first part of the recipe, with one face in front and one in back, but the necks are different. They are very long and are made of a special material: its qualities are extreme flexibility, strength and lightness. These necks are like a long column of liquid energy. They move easily and softly like the stem of an aquatic flower.

Close your eyes and remain motionless with your physical head.

Your four imaginary heads and necks, and eight faces with the sixteen paintbrushes, are in the same situation as in the first part of this recipe, with the sea and sky all around, below and above you.

Do the movements as described in the main directions for part I of this recipe

> with each head separately
>
> with each combination of pairs
>
> with each combination of three
>
> with all four

Your physical head remains motionless. Eyes are closed. Begin with one head, the one most natural to you.

You soon discover this fascinating fact: since these necks

are much *thinner* and *more pliable* than your ordinary neck and since there is no breastbone or backbone or shoulders, your paintbrushes can go much higher into the sky and deeper into the sea!!

If you find this recipe complicated and requiring close concentration and attention, I agree with you!! I too find it demanding! Do it only as long as you can do it with concentration. Two or three minutes of deep attention are more valuable than a long time with no attention.

If you wish to have a rest from the preceding, do the following.

Variation:

> You have only one head in addition to your own. Your imaginary head—with two faces and four paintbrushes—is located directly above your real head. The long neck of your imaginary head emerges from the top of your real head.
>
> With your imaginary head follow the directions given in part I for your real head, which is motionlessly poised in perfect balance on top of your spine.

If you can maintain concentration, I suggest giving either part of this recipe, or any of the variations, ten minutes a day for thirty days. The change in the feeling of neck and head is often remarkable. Movements made in the imagination are sometimes more beneficial than those done physically. In this recipe we work on both levels, and on the part of our body which is often in dire need of smoothing and attention.

Too often we get *it* in the neck!

Look at the windshield wiper on your car sweeping away again and again the incessantly falling drops of water in that heavy autumn rain. Again and again the blurred glass is made limpid and new. We are not windshield wipers nor is our life a car, and fortunately there is not always an autumn rain. But let us imagine a windshield wiper on the inside of our forehead: it cleans our bodymind of the droplets of unpleasantness, discord, useless suffering. Let our inner windshield wiper clear our vision so it will not be obscured by an accumulation of dust and mud through which the sun cannot shine—to us, from us.

NASA

"We look . . . something like an eclipse of the sun by the moon."

—Sheila Ostrander and Lynn Schroeder, *Psychic Discoveries Behind the Iron Curtain*

OUR BODY OF LIGHT

What is the aura? The dictionary gives the following definitions: (1) an invisible emanation; (2) an invisible atmosphere, supposedly arising from and surrounding a person or thing.

The word "invisible" is mentioned twice. But "invisible" is a subjective word. Invisible when? to whom? You and I are invisible to each other if we are in the dark or ten miles apart, but a cat or an eagle can see us.

A modern clairvoyant, Annie Besant, defines the aura this way: "What is called the aura of man is the outer part of the cloud-like substance of his higher bodies, interpenetrating each other and extending beyond the confines of his physical body, the smallest of all."* John Pierrakas, M.D., defines the aura as "a reflection of the energies of life processes."

The aura has been given many names:

electromagnetic field
energy body
etheric body

* *Thought Form*, Annie Besant. The Theosophical Publishing House, Madras and London, 1969.

double
unifying mechanism
the biological plasma body
pulsating energy body
star body
Body of Light

For these recipes we have chosen the name Body of Light.

When *Psychic Discoveries Behind the Iron Curtain* was published in 1970, it was considered so sensational that many people thought it was a swindle. In America that book gave a legitimate passport to the Body of Light to enter the universities; the study of extrasensory phenomena has now become an accepted realm for scientists.

An article in *Science News* entitled "Science Focuses on a 'Light of Life'" makes a comprehensive inquiry into Kirlian photography (also called radiation-field photography) and the study of the aura in American laboratories. Most scientists agree with Dr. Thelma Moss of U.C.L.A. that the aura or Body of Light "reveals enormous differences in energy states in individuals and this may have practical applications for treating diseases, alcoholics, for psychotherapy and for studying people interaction."* It is also valuable as a diagnostic tool because illness can be detected in our Body of Light before becoming obvious and advanced in our physical body. Just imagine the enormous advances in preventive medicine when one of the specializations in our medical schools becomes "aura diagnosis"! The acceptance and study of the Body of Light is now growing so fast that we may soon be speaking of aura-blind people, just as we do of the color-blind. (And a

* *Science News,* Vol. 104, September 29, 1973.

vitamin or enzyme may be offered as a cure for aura-blindness!)

It is likely that, as we achieve a real awareness of the pulsations and the changes in our Body of Light, we will also achieve a higher degree of direction over our moods, our health and the ways we relate to and influence our world.

"How is she today?"

"Her colors are lovely, except for the brown spot over her right hip. However, it is less dark than last week."

"I saw B.G., poor man. He is full of reddish streaks two or three feet long. If he doesn't change his mind, he is headed for a stroke."

What an enormous step could be made psychologically if we could see each other's Body of Light. How many games would crumple like empty balloons. If we could see, actually see with our own eyes, that the arrogant young man's emanations are those of a frightened child, that the bossy woman's Body of Light is that of a lonely, disappointed female, our behavior might change for the better. With the present quickening of scientific and experimental knowledge, extrasensory phenomena may soon be as familiar to us as electricity is. But we don't have to wait any longer. The following recipes will enhance our realization that we emit an invisible yet powerful energy of which we are often unaware.

Body of Light for One

Directions:

Sit in complete comfort in a place with a soothing light. Place the palms of your hands in front of you, facing each other, about one-half to one inch apart.

Keep your hands in that position for about two or three minutes. Although your hands do not touch each other, there is a communication between them. This may be a feeling of heat or coolness, of sparks of electricity shooting back and forth between the two hands.

After about three minutes, move your hands to and fro without letting them touch, increasing the distance between them from about one inch to two inches and, little by little, to three or four inches. The distance and the feeling vary with each individual. Some persons pull their hands apart as much as three feet and still feel electrical sparks going back and forth, or feel the stretching and shrinking of some strange kind of putty, jelly or taffy.

Our organism has a positive and negative current—the Chinese call it *yin* and *yang*. In this recipe we experience a meeting, possibly a balancing of the two currents.

In a matter of minutes, this recipe substantiates the Body of Light as factual rather than theoretical. Hours of discussion and reading might not achieve the same results. As you continue to feel the communication between your hands, you can pull them farther and farther apart and still feel a link—a sparking or a push and a pull—between them. In an even and dim light, or if you shade your light with cobalt-blue gelatin paper, you often see horizontal lines (of energy?) from one hand to the other. Whenever you feel restless or unbalanced, play with this recipe for fifteen or twenty minutes and the result will be a tranquil sense of vitality.

Caressing

Directions:

> After you have become aware of the energy between your hands, give your face a lovely massage.
>
> Put your hands about half an inch away from your face; begin at the chin and go slowly upward.
>
> Feel the vitalizing strokes of your hands going upward from the chin to the cheeks, eyes and forehead.
>
> Let your hands go upward past your hair, shake them lightly, begin again from the chin.

To your face this caress is the loving breeze in a summer night's dream.

Body of Light for Two

The following recipe is a variation of the preceding ones with a different flavor, since it is to be done with another person.

Richard Miller, physicist and Director of Research at the Department of Paraphysics and Parapsychology at the Experimental College in Seattle, has identified emissions from the human body as pheronomes (gases that contain communication signals). "Much human response could depend on the exchange of pheronomes," says Miller. "Of course this goes on at a subliminal level—below the level of conscious awareness."*

Directions:

> Face each other in a position comfortable enough to be held for a long time.
>
> Place one pair of hands horizontally above the other, about half to one full inch away, palms facing each other. (One pair of hands will be facing the ceiling and the other the floor.)

* *Science News*, Vol. 104, September 29, 1973.

Remain with the two pairs of hands facing each other, without touching, for about five minutes.

When you feel comfortable enough to hold that position for a while, close your eyes and just feel the energy of your partner. Feel this energy contact for several minutes.

Then one of you gives the direction: "Move up and down." Eyes remain closed.

The person whose hands are on top begins to move them slowly up and down, about one or two inches. Without looking, the person with the hands underneath follows the movement by following the emanation of the hands above.

Continue this for as long as you enjoy it, and feel the flow of energy. Its quality generally intensifies.

Then reposition the hands as in the beginning. One of you will now give the direction: "Move horizontally." Your eyes remain closed.

The lower hands begin to make slow horizontal movements, as the upper hands follow the energy emanating from the hands below. Before doing this be sure that the energy between the four hands is flowing.

After following the movement of your partner for about ten minutes, open your eyes and look at each other.

I have done this often with a group of people who had just met. The result amazes me every time; among the majority of couples a wordless communication, meaningful and surprising, is discovered. Experience this recipe with eyes closed and in silence.

If anyone is skeptical about the Body of Light for Two, it is best to do this recipe first; the discussion is more sophisticated when it follows the experience.

Your Body of Light*

Directions:

Make yourself comfortable and be sure you will not be disturbed for about one hour. You are going to create your own Body of Light.

See your Body of Light as a very small, perfectly proportioned replica of your physical body.

Your Body of Light is luminous.

It is located at the center of your physical body.

See this small, perfect Body of Light and feel it in the center of your being.

This Body of Light has your physical body features perfected to their highest expression of nobility and beauty.

The Body of Light which you create is your own unique body made perfect.

Create it in all details.

Your Body of Light is small, perfect, overwhelmingly intense, almost unbearably luminous.

---

* This is a spoken recipe, available on a long-playing record or tape, which can be obtained from "Recipes for Living & Loving," by Laura Huxley, 1540 Washburn Road, Pasadena, Calif. 91105.

Feel it and enjoy it as long as you wish.

After a while a change begins to take place: remaining perfectly proportioned and luminous, your Body of Light begins to expand. The expansion is like a flow of fresh energy: little by little your Body of Light seeps into every cell, every bone, every muscle, exuding a feeling of buoyancy and lightness. This Body of Light is permeating your physical body with tender, loving feeling.

When your Body of Light has reached a size comfortable to you, it stops expanding. All the while its radiance continues to bathe every muscle, every cell. Now this radiance is seeping through each pore of your skin—expanding out of you, creating a glow all around you, as in the illustration of the eclipse. This luminosity is expanding irresistibly all around you—pulsating deeply with life rhythm, tenderly touching and vitalizing everything, everyone near you.

As you walk in the streets, as you walk into a room, as you walk in the country, you feel this light within and all around you making contact a few instants before your physical body makes contact. People and animals feel this flow of loving energy emanating from you.

You touch without touching.

Like a shining, heralding archangel, your Body of Light announces you.

*We are going to be honored with the visit of a very emi-
nent guest: What shall we have for dinner?*

Menu

Course I	*Eleven abdominal breaths*
Course II	*Twenty-two lateral breaths*
Course III	*Thirty-three nostril-tasting breaths*
Course IV	*A few lip-tasting breaths*
Course V	*Fruits in season, harvested in the guest's presence*

BREATHE MORE
EAT LESS
LOVE MORE:

AN EPICUREAN RECIPE

Breathe More

Life is a constant struggle against oxygen deficiency.
—Ivan Petrovich Pavlov

The original meaning of the word "breath" is "psyche or mind or soul." We have spoken of breathing, yet the importance of breath-mind-soul compels me to accept the risk of repetition.

Breathing is:
both a conscious and an unconscious function—
a link between our conscious and our subconscious, which is one of the reasons some methods of meditation begin with breathing;
the uninterrupted flow by which our inner environment is externalized by exhaling, and our external environment is internalized by inhaling.

For thousands of years, breathing has been highly developed as a science by yogis, who are now being studied by Western scientists. In the West, a most important discovery in the medical field was made by the Nobel laureate Dr. Otto Warburg, Director of the Max Planck Institute for Cell Physiology in Berlin. In his famous Lindau lecture in 1969, he announced the discovery of the primary cause of all types of cancer. "Oxygen gas, the donor of energy in plants and animals, is dethroned in the cancer cells and replaced by energy-yielding reactions of the lowest living forms, namely, a fermentation of glucose."*

It is reported in the *Nature/Science Annual, 1974*** that Dr. Robert Rand, M.D., in collaboration with the Stanford Linear Accelerator Center, devised a method of killing cancer cells by depriving them of nourishment. These medical leaders have established that cancer cells die in an environment sufficiently saturated with oxygen. Other medical authorities have reported on the value of oxygen for a host of degenerative diseases other than cancer —arthritis, arteriosclerosis, and heart ailments are among them.

We maintain the oxygenation of our cells through specific nourishments, with certain enzymes, vitamins and minerals which promote absorption and utilization of oxygen. But every instant of our life our cells are given "mind or soul" by the air we breathe. Shortage of oxygen produces a destructive conversion in our cells, giving rise to grave illnesses. This evil cellular suffocation is caused by insufficient exhalation, with the result of keeping an overdose of carbon dioxide in the system. Why inflict upon ourselves the lethal punishment of carrying this pernicious debris within us?

---

* *The Prime Cause and Prevention of Cancer*, Otto Warburg.
** *Nature/Science Annual, 1974*. Time-Life Books.

The deficient breather retains stale air in his lungs and bronchial tubes, stealing the space needed for an intake of fresh air. This is why we repeatedly point out that the basic condition for good breathing is complete exhalation. When we say "breathe more," we really mean "exhale more." Exhale *every bit of air out of your system.* Then the rush of fresh air will take its natural course with an effortless independence.

There is a pleasant and clarifying way to do this breathing, as a lovely expression of your artistic self rather than an exercise. Invest a few dollars in a wind instrument that can be played easily. Mine, called *Flauto Magico,* has a keyboard like a piano with a range of one and a half octaves. It is generally easier to play this instrument than to whistle. From the moment you put the magic flute to your lips and blow, the sound is soft and gentle. Here is a way to practice exhalation as an artistic expression:

> Before starting to play:
>
>> Exhale totally.
>>
>> Remain empty.
>>
>> Let the air rush in.
>
> Do this three times. At the end of the third cycle when you are totally filled with air, put the instrument to your mouth and exhale into it while playing one note, a chord or a melodic phrase on the keyboard.
>
> Before taking another breath, use all of the air in your lungs—every bit of it—to play as you like. Hold the note a long time, as if to gently stretch it without breaking it. To do this, play very softly, giving your air out ever so slowly, making it last for an uninterrupted, drawn-out, soft flow of sound. Gradually release all the air in your long musical projection. It is lovely to make a tender

pianissimo last longer and longer, until it fades away into silence.

When your air is totally expended, refill yourself to capacity, without taking your mouth away from the instrument, inhaling through the nose as much air as you can take in. Feel it filling your abdomen and chest, lifting your breast (not your shoulders), passing through your throat. With this air you will make music, and while so delightfully engaged, you use creatively the energy contained in stale air, retention of which would defile your bodymind.

See how long you can sustain a melody, chord or note.

Listen to the fascinating sound of a single note—the note *you* are creating.

Find the note to which your whole being resonates. Discover your own sound: its vibrations are your vibrations. Meet yourself in that sound.

You can increase and decrease the volume, initiating your sound so tenderly that it can hardly be heard—make it rise in intensity as the sun rises at dawn; make it dissolve as imperceptibly as a pale moon vanishes in the morning mist. All the while you are converting devitalized air into sound and music. What a supreme alchemist you are!

Eat Less

Contrary to the general impression derived from the use of the word "epicurean," the Greek philosopher Epicurus (342–270 B.C.) lived a very simple life. His diet was barley bread and water, and a half pint of wine occasionally was held to be ample allowance. He wrote to a correspondent, "Send me some Cynthian cheese so that, should I choose, I may fare sumptuously."

Epicurus believed our universe to be only one of an innumerable variety of worlds in infinite space, and that these worlds may have systems very different from our own. As modern physics did twenty-three centuries later, Epicurus promulgated abolition of the dualism between mind and matter. He was the head of a peaceful community believing in the oneness of body and soul, the soul being a finer species of body, permeating our bodily frame. It was the refinement of his perception that gave him the pleasure of "faring sumptuously" on a piece of cheese, barley bread and a half pint of wine. Epicurus believed that pleasure is to be cultivated as a lofty way of life, as a habit of mind. But he wrote, "We cannot live pleasantly without living wisely and nobly . . ."

This recipe is for those who embrace this life style and whose perceptions have become acute enough to derive pleasure from simple things. Because you eat less, you must choose the best, the most genuine, the freshest of foods—foods that are unpolluted, raw or lightly cooked. It must be *live* food, and cannot therefore be canned, frozen, cellophaned or otherwise packed, pickled, reconstructed, reinforced, etc. See boxes, cans and packages as the coffins of the food they contain. The best food is often the least expensive because it has not been manufactured, stored, transported for thousands of miles and advertised—procedures which involve the greatest part of each dollar you spend for your "nutrition."

It is a mistake to change your diet too quickly and drastically. Take your time. Each week decide to eliminate one of the dead foods you may normally consume, and in its place substitute one which is more alive. For instance, if you eat canned or frozen vegetables, substitute a fresh vegetable. If you eat dead pie, change to living fruits. If you eat commercial breakfast food, buy a whole-grain cereal (millet, whole wheat, whole oats, barley, etc.) . Abrupt changes are difficult for some of us, so make the change at your own pace, even if it takes several months.

As you change the quality, you will also be able to change the quantity of the food you eat. A single slice of genuine bread, made with a few basic ingredients, will satisfy you more than five slices of fake bread. It is also better to eat a small quantity of a new food with awareness; chew the first five bites about fifty times each. Cultivate your taste buds; give all three thousand of them the chance to feel the mildness and sharpness, temperature and texture of your food, as well as its weight and fluidity. If you eat in this way it is quite certain that you will not be choked to death by "inhalation of food." It is reported by the National Safety Council that every year 2,500 persons in the United States die in the course of a meal, suffocated by food going into the windpipe; this is the sixth most frequent cause of accidental death. Take the same amount of time to eat an orange which you formerly took to eat two. Note the inextricable connection of taste and smell, and realize what the look of your food does to your palate.

Directions:

Approach this recipe, not as a martyr, but as an Epicurean.

Choose fresh food; enjoy buying and looking at it.

Keep the first five mouthfuls in your mouth for a long time to extract full pleasure and better nutrition.

Give ten minutes, twice a day, to play your chosen note or melody, or alternatively, one hour to energetic walking, dancing or any exercise promoting complete exhalation, which is an essential part of food assimilation.

Be particularly attentive to elimination: through your lungs, as described in "Breathe More"; through your skin by self-massage with a rough towel; and through your kidneys and colon. Study the incredible ability of the small and large intestines to absorb nourishment and eliminate waste. What comes out of you is as important to your well-being as what goes in.

Diminish the quantity and improve the quality of your food gradually as you develop your capacity to extract more nutritional pleasure from the food you eat. Make this interesting change a project of your own—no need to rush.

Dr. Alexander Comfort, international authority on aging, reports: "You need only feed mice and rats two days and starve them the third day to double their life span without restricting their growth at all. . . . There is evidence for every organism that it has been tried on, that it works."*

* *Center Report*, Center for the Study of Democratic Institutions, Santa Barbara, Calif., June 1974.

Love More

"Love more" is the imploring command given us by saints and sages of all times and places. We all know that this is the solution—the only solution. "One never loves enough." The shortage of love in the world is the major cause of food starvation and—yes—of oxygen starvation.

How is love starvation connected with food starvation? The fact is that famine is due as much to food distribution as to food shortage. Millions are dying because they have too little to eat—millions are dying because they have too much to eat.

Basically it is ignorance and greed that have caused this tragic situation.

When their words were unheard or misinterpreted, Christ, Gandhi, Chavez, Dolci and other love-inspired leaders undertook long fasts in order to make their point clear to their people and to the world.

A long fast by a person who knows *how* to fast frequently puts him into a state of expanded consciousness, giving him a more direct and deeper level of communication with the masses, confused by propaganda but clearminded about hunger. Gandhi's forty-day fast prepared him to face the mighty British Empire, which eventually bowed to the emaciated, powerful Indian leader. The severe fasting of great saints has brought food and work to multitudes. Those of us who are not saints will enjoy Epicurean eating in many ways—one of them being the knowledge that, by increasing the world's food supply, we improve the human condition.

It takes only a moment's thought to see how oxygen starvation and love starvation are closely related. When we are relaxed and secure, loving and loved, our breathing is vastly different from when we are in a toxic state of bodymind. When we are nervous, fearful or angry, we hold our breath; in deep depression and catatonia breathing is reduced to a minimum. It is obvious that we suspend the inhalation of oxygen and exhalation of carbon dioxide in tense situations. Just recall any difficult examination, or a confrontation, or a moment of danger when driving, or the receipt of bad news about someone you love—you almost stop breathing.

We all have moments of light or severe trauma when our breathing is reduced to a minimum. The problem is that we are often frozen in these moments for the rest of our lives; the result is easy to see. How many people do you know whose bodily posture is not, in some measure, distorted? This distortion inhibits proper breathing, causing a damaging shortage of our primal necessity: oxygen. Oxygen, food and love are part of the life chain—when one link is weakened through deprivation, its functioning as a whole is impaired. Sometimes, in spite of all shortages and deprivations, a sweeping wave of love miraculously balances and illuminates everything, lifts us out of ourselves, and shows the miserly limitation of our logical thinking. While trusting in these triumphant manifestations of a higher reality, we also acknowledge the fact that a minimum fulfillment of bodily need is generally necessary for love to remain present.

What are the benefits we derive from a balanced fusion of oxygen, food and love?

Food will be available to millions of us presently starving.

We will use our money and energy which are presently spent to care for illness due to starvation or to overeating, underbreathing and underloving, for pleasurable, educational endeavors.

Improvement in our general well-being enlivens our will to good and will to beauty, thus eliminating many of the causes of personal conflict and impersonal, subhuman war.

Are these sufficient reasons to

Breathe More   *Eat Less*   *Love More?*

As I am ending this book I find a birthday greeting of a few years ago from Ginny, to whom this book is dedicated. Her seemingly paradoxical message is the best life plan I can leave with you. She wrote:

"We all love you more than we can."

APPENDIX ONE

APPENDIX TWO

SUGGESTED READINGS

APPENDIX ONE

Project Sanity

"So there is no panacea?"
"How could there be?"
. . . There is no single cure for what can never have a single cause.

Aldous wrote and developed this theme in *Island* and other books.

The information I am about to give you is no panacea. But it has alleviated the guilt of many parents who thought the erratic behavior of their children was due to faulty upbringing. It has liberated great numbers of people from confinement in mental institutions. It has lifted the elderly from the distressing feeling of losing their mental capacities. The treatment is called Orthomolecular Therapy.

Through Aldous's interest in education and medicine, and his admiration for the independent and creative thinking of scientific pioneers, I have had the privilege of receiving this information directly, from the beginning and from its source. Although this professional knowledge, being of a medical nature, may not belong in this book, I would be humanistically neglectful were I not to give it exposure.

The acceptance of this treatment by the medical community has been slow, as it usually is with a new approach, even when as safe as this. However, at this writing it is estimated that in the past twenty years about thirty thousand persons have benefited. Recognition and application by the medical profession are quickly increasing as patients' reports of their newly found reason for living create interest and demand.

Very briefly, this is the history of Orthomolecular treatment:

In 1952 at Weyburn Hospital in Saskatchewan, Canada, Dr. Abram Hoffer (Director of Research in Psychiatry in the Department of Public Health) and Dr. Humphrey Osmond (Professor of Psychiatry, University of Alabama Medical School, and Consultant in Psychiatry to Bryce Hospital) dedicated themselves to the study of mental disease—especially schizophrenia and alcoholism. The result was one of the most beneficent discoveries in this field: they found that in many cases the schizophrenia and related mental disturbances were *not* due to psychological causes but to a nutritional shortage arising from an inborn characteristic which prevents the body from absorbing certain vitamins and minerals from food. The treatment for this abnormality is to provide these vitamins (especially vitamin B₃, also called niacin, niacinimide, nicotinamide or nicotinic acid) in amounts vastly larger than those generally needed. Dr. Linus Pauling, twice a Nobel prize winner, conducting independent research in molecular biochemistry, confirmed and amplified the work of Dr. Hoffer and Dr. Osmond, and named this new branch of medicine "Orthomolecular Psychiatry."

"We all practice what Dr. Pauling has described as orthomolecular psychiatry, the provision of essential nutrients to people who lack them," says Dr. Hoffer.*

Essential nutrients are water, protein, fats, vitamins, minerals and oxygen, which in turn prevent or facilitate the manufacture of other chemicals (enzymes, hormones, etc.) by our bodymind. Mental and physical disturbances of various kinds and intensity occur when there is too much or too little of one or more of those nutrients.

In 1927 Freud foresaw the advent of Orthomolecular Psychiatry: "I am firmly convinced that one day all these disturbances we are trying to understand will be treated by means of hormones or similar substances." Twenty-five years later Drs. Hoffer, Osmond and Pauling discovered these substances. However, providing these substances does not imply in any way that emotional support, psychotherapy, meditation, self-expression, etc., are unnecessary. On the contrary, they are as important to the Orthomolecular treatment as to any other.

"At the beginning," says Dr. Hoffer, "we concentrated on schizophrenia and alcoholism, but in the last five years the spectrum has expanded; it covers hyperkinetic or overactive children with learning disabilities, disturbed adolescents, drug problems, adult schizophrenia, memory loss and problems of old age."

Evidence is quickly increasing that Orthomolecular treatment, in connection with others, is one of the most

* *Doctors Speak on the Ortho-Molecular Approach.* Available through the Huxley Institute for Biosocial Research, 1114 First Avenue, New York, N.Y. 10021; or the Canadian Schizophrenic Foundation, #10–1630 Albert Street, Regina, Saskatchewan, Canada.

efficient and least expensive means to ameliorate the number-one health problem in America: mental illness.

Note: The Huxley Institute for Biosocial Research (named for biologist Sir Julian Huxley and his brother Aldous) is offering a pilot medical training course for selected physicians, psychiatrists and neurologists with the hope that this treatment will be made available to the rural and urban poor. For information, contact the Institute.

APPENDIX TWO:

Project Caressing

.

LONELINESS

ALIENATION

SEPARATENESS

ISOLATION

We hear their voices—loud or soft, plaintive or irate, timid or demanding—at ever-increasing tempo, in an ever-deepening intensity. When these voices reach their climax we hear only the dead silence of apathy.

It is at the two extremes of life that loneliness is most acutely felt—for in the years between, action and involvement absorb our time and energy. Many are the causes of loneliness. One has been established by the behavioral scientists beyond any hope of doubt; the child that is not fondled and caressed in his first two years of life will become neurotic, or miasmic, or unresponsive, or autistic, or delinquent, or underachieving—the problem being determined by genes or culture. Each of these afflictions generates isolation and loneliness. A friend of mine traveling in Mexico saw a beautiful child and asked his mother's permission to photograph him. She was pleased by the request but when the photographer was leaving she stopped him and said, "Touch him," and then she added, "A child that is not touched will be unlucky." This Mexican mother expressed, in another way, the same obvious fact that modern science has proved.

The most deeply felt communication an infant has with the outer world is through the skin. For the nine months of gestation, he feels no boundaries between his body and that of his mother. The shock of birth is partly due to that separation: suddenly alone in an incomprehensible, possibly inimical universe, he longs for and needs one thing more than any other—skin contact. This has been dramatically illustrated by Dr. Harris F. Harlow, who found in experiments with baby monkeys that the baby would relinquish food almost completely—eating the absolute minimum to keep alive from a mechanical source—and would pass his time nestling against the imitation monkey, whose softness gave it some resemblance to a live monkey.

And what about the other age of loneliness, when a person young in body and spirit finds himself obliged to retire professionally? He could enter a period of challenging exploration in work, study and styles of life he never had the opportunity to experience before. However, many do not take advantage of this opportunity. They find themselves alienated from their families and often give up their homes to live in groups and loneliness. Trying to fill the gap between past and future, they forget that they have only the present. These people can look forward to one beautiful opportunity of here-and-now involvement: CARESSING.

For "Project Caressing" I envisage in every city block

a serene, soundproof, pastel-colored room, furnished only with comfortable rocking armchairs and pillows. In this room the new and the old loneliness meet and dissolve. The adult participators would give an hour or more of their time to *hold a baby*, knowing that their warmth and affection will magically infuse the child's entire life with responsive tenderness. No words will interfere with the soft melting of loneliness into silent loving communication: only soothing humming in the "Caressing Room," or golden silence. For in the world of the infant it is the contact with a living body and with a beating heart that counts—not contact with incomprehensible words, or with those wretched plastic bassinets that substitute for embracing arms. The busy mothers and fathers will be able to leave the infant in the "Caressing Room" knowing that only affection and tranquillity will be given, rather than the catastrophic noises, lights, radiations and vibrations of television, so often used as a built-in, never-quiet, never-caring baby sitter. And the older people, who more and more are becoming separated from their grandchildren, will feel the joy of giving—not money or work or things—but giving themselves and their love for the sheer pleasure of it. They will *hold a baby*, feel his pure tender skin, and by the magic of touching they will be touched.

The urgency of "Project Caressing" cannot be overemphasized. It is sufficient to see the statistics on "battered" (a polite word for tortured) children, on neurotic adolescents, on people of all ages dependent on psychiatric care, on the number of children waiting to find a foster home. A recent article posed the question "Motherhood —Who Needs It?" Ask the children. Project Caressing will be outdated only when our society becomes so enlightened as to take the birth of a new human being as the most important happening of the society—a happening for which a man and a woman and the group they live in will prepare physically and emotionally, with intelligence and love. Then we will have a race for which love is living and each breath is a caress. Certainly the actualization of such an idea will take thought, money, organization and overcoming of obstacles. However much it takes, it will be a thousand times less money, energy and time than it takes to produce a single hydrogen bomb, which is constructed for the purpose of perpetuating a chain reaction of hate.

Again, it is our choice whether to support a chain reaction of death and hate, or one of life and love.

SUGGESTED READING

Abrahamson, E. M., and A. W. Pezet: *Body, Mind and Sugar* (New York: Pyramid Publications, 1971).

Adams, Murray: *Megavitamin Therapy* (New York: Larchmont Books, 1973).

Airola, Paavo O.: *Are You Confused?* (Health Plus Publications, 1971)

Al Chung-liang Huang: *Embrace Tiger, Return to Mountain: The Essence of T'ai Chi* (New York: Bantam Books, 1975).

Assagioli, Roberto: *The Act of Will* (New York: Penguin Books, 1974).

———: *Psychosynthesis* (New York: Compass Books, Viking Press, 1971).

Blaine, Tom R.: *Mental Health Through Nutrition* (New Jersey: Citadel Press, 1969).

Cheraskin, E., and M. Ringsdorf: *New Hope for Incurable Disease* (Hicksville, N.Y.: Exposition–University Press, 1971).

Cooper, Kenneth: *New Aerobics* (New York: Bantam Books, 1970).

Dass, Ram: *Be Here Now* (New York: Crown Publishers, 1971).

———: *The Only Dance There Is* (New York: Anchor Press, Doubleday, 1974).

Davis, Adelle: *Let's Get Well* (New York: Harcourt Brace Jovanovich, 1965).

de Mille, Richard: *Put Your Mother on the Ceiling* (New York: Walker, 1967).

de Sainte Colombe, Paul: *Grapho Therapeutics: Pen and Pencil Therapy* (New York: Popular Library, 1973).

Feldenkrais, Moshe: *Awareness Through Movement* (New York: Harper & Row, 1972).

Hauser, Gayelord: *Gayelord Hauser's New Treasury of Secrets* (New York: Farrar, Straus & Giroux, 1974).

Hudson, Thomson Jay: *The Law of Psychic Phenomena* (New York: Samuel Weiser, 1970).

Huxley, Aldous: *The Art of Seeing* (Seattle, Washington: Montana Books, 1975).

———: *Collected Essays* (New York: Harper & Row, 1971).

———: *Island* (New York: Harper & Row, 1962).

Lilly, John: *The Center of the Cyclone* (New York: Julian Press, 1972).

Lowen, Alexander: *Depression and the Body* (New York: Coward, McCann & Geoghegan, 1972).

Mensendieck, Bess M.: *Look Better, Feel Better* (New York: Harper & Row, 1954).

Perls, F. S.: *Ego, Hunger and Aggression:* The Beginning of Gestalt Therapy (New York: Random House, 1969).

Pfeiffer, Carl: *Schizophrenias, Yours and Mine* (New York: Pyramid Publications, 1970).

Ramecharaka, Yogi: *Hatha Yoga* (Des Plaines, Illinois: Yoga Publications Society).

Reps, Paul, ed.: *Zen Flesh Zen Bone: A Collection of Zen and Pre-Zen Writings* (New York: Anchor Press, Doubleday).

Roberts, Sam E.: *Exhaustion: Causes and Treatment* (New York: Rodale Press, 1967).

Samuels, Mike, and Hal Z. Bennett: *Be Well* (New York: Random House, 1974).

Shattock, E. H.: *An Experiment in Mindfulness* (New York: Samuel Weiser, 1958).

Shelton, Herbert: *Fasting Can Save Your Life* (Chicago, Illinois: Natural Hygiene Press, 1974).

Stone, Irwin: *The Healing Factor: Vitamin C Against Disease* (New York: Grosset and Dunlap, 1972) .

Wen-Shan Huang: *Fundamentals of Tai Chi Ch'uan* (American Academy of Chinese Culture, dist., 1974) .

Williams, Roger: *Nutrition against Disease* (New York: Bantam Books, 1971) .

————: *Nutrition in a Nutshell* (New York: Dolphin Books, Doubleday, 1962) .

————: *You Are Extraordinary* (New York: Random House, 1967) .

Wu Ch'eng-en: *Monkey,* translated by Arthur Waley (New York: Grove Press, 1958) .

LAURA ARCHERA HUXLEY

"A succession of explorations and discoveries—that is what my life has been," says Laura Archera Huxley, whose life continues to be a series of investigations uncovering answers for her ceaseless questions about the nature and quality of life.

Laura has indeed undergone a series of discoveries throughout the course of her life. From the age of ten, she lived and moved in the universe of the violin, going from her native Turin, Italy, to study with the masters in Berlin, Paris, and Rome, where she earned a Professor of Music degree. She made her teenage debut in Carnegie Hall, continuing her music education at the Curtis Institute of Philadelphia. At this point, Laura decided she knew little of life other than that of the concert violinist. After a long and painful deliberation, she put her Guarneri into its case and set out to discover wider horizons.

During the following years, she produced film documentaries, played in a major symphony orchestra, and intensively studied health, nutrition, and psychology.

The common denominator that impressed her in all her activities was the problem of human relations. The vast amount of avoidable unhappiness with which people are affected presented a challenge to which the Recipes for Living and Loving in *You Are Not the Target* (1963) and *Between Heaven and Earth* (1975) are the response.

In 1956, Laura married Aldous Huxley. Together they explored ways of opening the mind to new levels of consciousness. Since her husband's death on November 22, 1963, she has continued to expand her eclectic approach to the provocative enigma of human potentialities.

In 1978, Laura founded *Our Ultimate Investment*, an organization for the nurturing of the "Possible Human", beginning before conception.

"The unjust and frightening question whether to abort or not to abort must be changed to 'Should I conceive or not conceive,'" states Huxley. "Unless we make that change, mindless violence will continue and the realization of our potentialities for intelligence and compassion will proceed at a snail-like pace because of the unconsciously inflicted damage to the human being at the time of conception—and thereafter."

She currently lives in Los Angeles with her granddaughter Karen, whom she adopted as a baby and who is now sixteen.

If you would like to receive a catalog of Hay House products, or information about future workshops, lectures, and events sponsored by the Louise L. Hay Educational Institute, please detach and mail this questionnaire.

Thank you for ordering *Between Heaven and Earth*. Please fill out this questionnaire to help us serve you better. In return, we will send you a catalog of our current products.

NAME_____

ADDRESS_____

_____

I purchased this book from

    Store_____

    City_____

    Other (Catalog, Lecture, Workshop)_____

Occupation_____ Age_____

Other topics you would enjoy:_____

Thank you for ordering *Between Heaven and Earth*. Please fill out this questionnaire to help us serve you better. In return, we will send you a catalog of our current products.

NAME_____

ADDRESS_____

_____

I purchased this book from

    Store_____

    City_____

    Other (Catalog, Lecture, Workshop)_____

Occupation_____ Age_____

Other topics you would enjoy:_____